SNOW-SHOEING

THIRD EDITION

GENE PRATER

THE MOUNTAINEERS / SEATTLE

The Mountaineers: Organized 1906 "... to explore, study, preserve, and enjoy the natural beauty of the Northwest."

Published by The Mountaineers
1011 S.W. Klickitat Way, Suite 107, Seattle, Washington 98134

Published simultaneously in Canada by Douglas & McIntyre, Ltd.
1615 Venables Street, Vancouver, B.C. V5L 2H1

6 5 4 3 2
5 4 3 2

Manufactured in the United States of America

Edited by Christine Deavel
Book design by Constance Bollen
Cover design by Betty Watson
Illustrations by Richard Pargeter, Marge Mueller and Nick Gregoric
Photos by the author
Cover photograph by Tom Kirkendall

Library of Congress Cataloging-in-Publication Data

Prater, Gene.
Snowshoeing.

Bibliography: p.
Includes index.
1. Snowshoes and snowshoeing. I. Title.
GV853.P72 1988 796.9'6 88-24452
ISBN 0-89886-178-0 (pbk.)

Contents

Preface

"Those are funny looking things on your feet. What do you use them for?"

"These are snowshoes. They have a light frame with webbing or decking laced to it. I strap them to my boots and they are large enough so I can walk on the snow without sinking very deep. It's kind of dismal and depressing to be stuck indoors all winter. I really enjoy a snow hike to remind me that my world doesn't shrink down to surfaced roads and cities just because there's some snow on the ground."

Snowshoers are always explaining what snowshoes are. Laced wood frame snowshoes have been around for centuries, but some explanation is helpful when you see what I call Western-type snowshoes for the first time. Metal frames and solid decking are a change from the traditional construction and materials.

Experienced snowshoers are fountains of wisdom about how to get around in the rugged backcountry as well. Countless times the same jewels of advice are repeated: "Say, if you kick your snowshoes deeper so the traction bites in, you won't slip." Or, "Why don't you take it easier? Often a little finesse is better than brute strength and muscle on snow." It seemed reasonable to me to collect all these jewels and put them in one place.

Recreational snowshoeing today is different from the original uses of snowshoes by the native North American, and from the uses by the trapper you envision snowshoeing along a trapline in the north woods. Generally speaking, traditional snowshoe designs work best in gentle terrain. New Englanders, however, use small snowshoes with flat toes for their steepest climbing. But for steep country everywhere, the more recent Western design is replacing the old wood models.

Don't misinterpret what I say. As I travel in the Snow Belt, I do see Western snowshoes being used more and more in territory where once only pre-1970s wood frame laced snowshoes were seen. However, there are vast, gentler areas where the traditional models are still in the majority.

Sales figures for snowshoes are difficult to find, but the best available to me at present may be of interest to the reader. Laced wood frame snowshoes made in the U.S. number 25,000 or so sales per year. Imports—mostly from Canada—are about the same, 20,000. Western snowshoes sell 10,000 to 12,000 pair per year. Of surprise to those people who favor Westerns is the figure of 50–60% of the 55,000 or so that are laced with rawhide. The Canadian market has been reported around 250,000 pairs per year for many years.

As I travel to different areas of the North American snowbelt and snowshoe with the local experts, I observe new or different techniques. This third edition includes many additions to the original *Snowshoeing*. It's easier to learn a new skill or activity if someone helps you take the first steps. The simplest binding looks like a tangle at first glance. The purpose of this little book is to encourage you to not only become a beginner but to continue on to a high level of expertise. There are numerous books telling about the easy parts of snow hiking or camping. I hope the information in this volume will help when winter travel is difficult.

Commercial products are treated equally in this book, in that trade names are avoided. Generic terms are used whenever possible to help a beginner choose equipment that is of good quality and works well in winter, without promoting sales of a particular make. To do so would be contrary to the policy of The Mountaineers and create doubts about the objectivity of the book. Furthermore, it is still possible that an adept and perceptive snowshoer can make a home workshop snowshoe as good as, if not better than, anything on the market now.

When I took my first steps on snowshoes, solitude began about a quarter mile from any road. Things have changed in the nearly 40 years since that experience. The outdoors—summer or winter—has been "sold" to the outdoor-oriented public as beneficial to health if not the solution to mankind's age-old problems of self-confidence and love of one's neighbors. A lot more people are out playing in the snow, and popular places may be crowded on weekends now.

Reach out to help beginners feel at home in the winter landscape. Most of us live and work in impersonal cities or suburbs where people don't want to get to know each other very well. It can add enjoyment to a winter outing to reverse this ethic and enjoy the warmth of human companionship.

As the years fly by I notice some gaps in the circle of outdoor-type friends I have enjoyed over the past 40 years. I have benefitted from many friendships and certain people made otherwise mediocre outings noteworthy and even outstanding. Memories of these friends now gone are still vivid because we walked or worked together side by side. Their special personalities are tied to a certain place and time, adding life and vitality to experiences that otherwise would fade as the years pass. Even when I hike by myself, I am not alone: through the medium of memory, I see in the sunset the faces of special friends and hear their voices in the wind.

I wish to thank the following people for providing information for this book: Don Anderson, Frank Ashley, Candice and George Bosworth, Joel Braatz, Joan Brady, Fred Camphausen, Jim and Ann Cody, Roy Harniss, Trudy Healy, Buck Hulse, Tim Kneeland, Jerry Koch, Serge Lebell, Kathie Le Clair, Vince Lee, Rob Newcomb, Bill Prater, Glenn Prozak, Bill and Virginia Swim, Dick Tucker, Jim Tucker, Laura and Gary Waterman, Dyke Williams, and Norman Wilson.

And special thanks to my editor, Christine Deavel, who put a polish and shine on my disorganized and rough manuscript.

I encourage you to get out in winter and learn to enjoy the woods and mountains for their qualities of beauty, solitude, and grandeur, and to take time to make friends with the people who share the adventure with you. Don't be deluded into thinking it's the fashionable clothing you wear or the speed of your oversnow travel device that provides the pleasure. It isn't. The outstanding part of your outing, the part that is memorable and enduring, is the backcountry and the good companions who accompany you.

My best for a great winter experience.

Above tree line in Montana's Beartooth Mountains

SECTION 1

Equipment

CHAPTER 1

The Snowshoe

No one knows for sure when the first snowshoe was devised. The wood-frame, rawhide-laced models we now regard as "old" or "original" designs are modern when compared with even earlier examples. Archaeological evidence indicates that the forerunner of the laced snowshoe was a solid slab of wood. This is a crude device compared with the museum-piece snowshoe, finely crafted of straight-grain wood and lacing as delicate as a crocheted tablecloth.

The earliest examples of solid-slab snowshoes are from central Asia. Perhaps some of these snowshoes were carried across the Aleutian land bridge by migrants to North America. Ancestors of the Eskimos and Indians of present Alaska and Canada modified the solid slab to the frame and laced snowshoes still used today.

Although differences among the early designs were likely adaptations to terrain—each shape meeting certain conditions of local environment—difference for its own sake was probably a consideration, too, as it still is among manufacturers of snowshoes. Animals with feet adapted to oversnow travel provided examples: beavertail snowshoes are shaped like the hind feet of the snowshoe rabbit and bearpaw models are quite like bobcat and lynx tracks. (The bear itself leaves much deeper tracks than the cats and prefers hibernation to snow travel.)

The natives of Canada and Alaska brought the snowshoe to its greatest height of craftsmanship as an object of beauty as well as a useful tool for survival. The wood frames with animal-hide webbing have an overall similarity, with individual differences. Most have one-piece frames, carefully tapered and bent

Ridgetop and rock tower, Lassen Volcanic National Park, California

to form. Some snowshoes are works of art, with a very fine lacing much too delicate to use for heavy packing in rugged mountain conditions. Perhaps these were "dress" snowshoes worn for show as cowboys wear 'dress boots" to town.

Most wood-frame snowshoes are similar in design, with an outside frame and one or more wood crosspieces to help hold the shape (Figure 1). The few that do not use crosspieces have heavier, stronger frames. White ash, an eastern wood, is the choice of most manufacturers for frames; by steaming or soaking in a special chemical bath, it can be bent without cracking and will hold the bends indefinitely. (But check for cracks before buying, and be sure both snowshoes match in size and shape.) Tightly stretched webbing plus the weight of the wearer tends to pull the sides of the frames together. The webbing is laced in a triangular system, with a heavily reinforced toe cord or binding hinge where the binding is attached. Lacing patterns may vary slightly, but all are basically similar. Thicker, heavier lacing is used for the section under the foot than for the toe and tail parts. Lacing used in colder areas where there is consistent powder snow is thinner than that used south of the U.S.-Canadian border where the wetter snow rapidly destroys lightweight lacing.

Traditionally, wood-frame snowshoes have been manufactured in the eastern United States and in Quebec, Canada. During World War II the demand for snowshoes apparently increased; many military surplus webs show trademarks from Michigan and Arkansas as well as the East.

Now, practically all wood-frame snowshoes are made in the eastern regions of both the United States and Canada. Metal-frame models were developed almost entirely in mountains near the West Coast, but the largest manufacturer has moved east from Washington to Wisconsin.

Basic Types

For simplicity, I classify snowshoe types into four basic categories: Yukon, beavertail, bearpaw, and Western (Figure 2). Sizes overlap and regional names are profuse and contradictory, but for general purposes the four-design description is adequate.

The **Yukon**, or **trail**, is about 10 inches wide and from 42 to 62 inches in length. Most have a very high toe turnup, to six or eight inches. Traditionally, these are best in open country and deep powder snow. The narrow width also makes them good for traversing slopes and the best type for descending steep slopes in soft snow. Their high toes ride up out of the snow and seldom catch on anything. However, the over-50-inch length and heavy weight make Yukons unwieldy for maneuvering in tight quarters, and the high toe can't be kicked into the snow to climb (step kicking), so these are not for mountain travel.

The **beavertail** has such local names as Maine, Michigan, and Huron. Sizes range from 9 × 30 inches to 20 × 44 inches, with 12 × 34 inches or so probably the most popular. Generally, they are almost flat and have a long tail. The flat toes make these the best for step kicking and are the favorite with eastern climbers for use in tough snowshoeing conditions. Widths of 12 inches and over are poor for sidehilling (traveling across a slope) but give the desired flotation in powder snow. The trade-off is often worth it, since snowshoers in the East seem to go straight up hills much more often than across them. Despite the width, beavertails have an overlapping pattern on

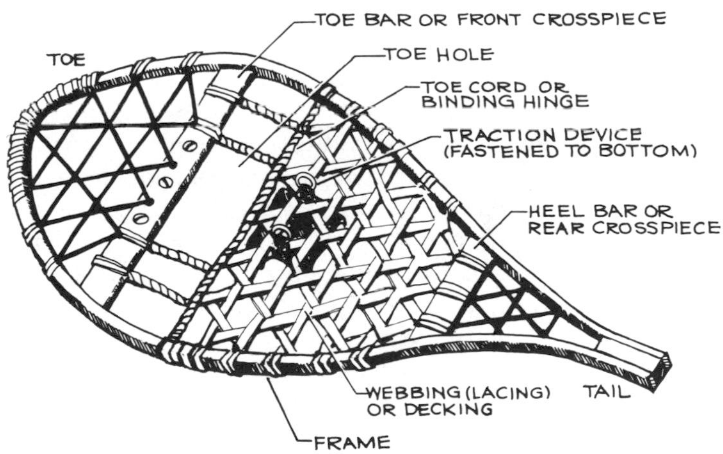

Fig. 1. The parts of a snowshoe

the trail (Figure 2), which is helpful when following a trail-breaker who is wearing narrower snowshoes.

Bearpaws, as the name implies, are short and wide, with rounded tails. Sizes range from 12 × 24 inches to 19 × 26 inches and 15 × 33 inches. Some have been modified to 10 × 36 inches. The most common size is probably 12 or 13 inches wide by 28 inches long. Thus they are rather rounded and usually flat, which makes them one of the best for kicking steps. The shorter length ensures easy maneuvering, although the width of 12 inches and over is a drawback on sidehills of squeezing between trees.

The flat toes of bearpaws will run under the surface during a steep descent, although lengths of 28 inches or shorter may be "heeled in" to kick steps on the way down. This can be a great advantage when you are descending very steep slopes in powder snow and can counteract the tendency of the flat toes to run under and trip you. Some people feel the rounded tails cause more drag than a snowshoe with a narrow, pointed tail. Lacing at the rear must be reinforced heavily because it abrades rapidly on a hard crust or in wet spring snow that has many sharp ice crystals in it.

First developed in the 1950s, **Western** snowshoes were modified in the 1970s and since have become a favorite with many snowshoers. They are smaller snowshoes, usually with a high toe turnup and a short toe section, made with aluminum frames and a synthetic decking that is laced or riveted to the frame and replaces the lacing (webbing). Sizes typically range from 8 × 22 inches to 9 × 38 inches. The frames, made of aluminum tubing or angle or I-beam aluminum, commonly include a crosspiece combined with a binding hinge, which functions as the toe cord on laced snowshoes. The metal binding hinge provides precise control of the snowshoe, allowing almost no lateral slack between the boot and the snowshoe. A serrated cleat of angle aluminum is attached to the crosspiece to increase traction (Figure 2).

At present, all models of Western snowshoes have factory-equipped bindings that are bolted or riveted to the snowshoe and are not interchangeable with other Western bindings. One model's hinge is attached to the frame with wide neoprene straps. This allows some flex or give, taking some strain off the frames and allowing the traction device to sink more deeply into the snow than devices on snowshoes with a rigid crosspiece.

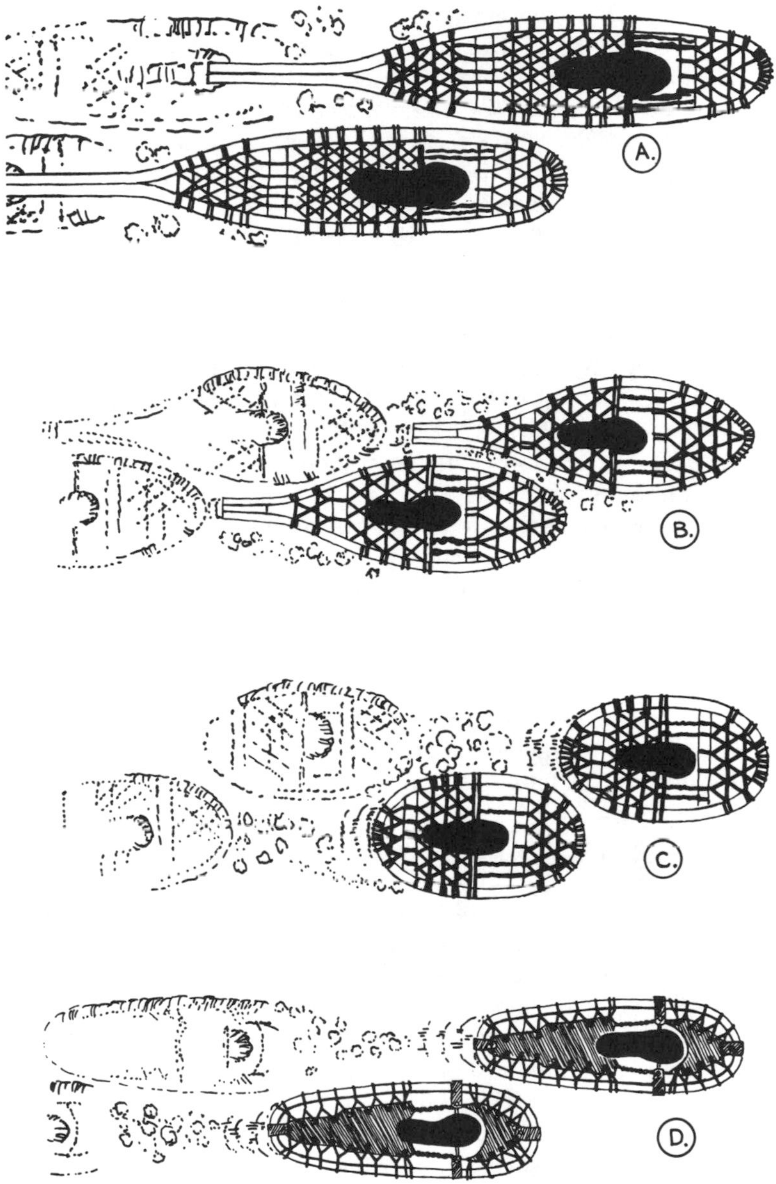

Fig. 2. Types of snowshoes: A. Yukon, B. Beavertail, C. Bearpaw, D. Western

Western snowshoes were designed in the West for mountain use. Their light weight and excellent binding and traction have combined to give outstanding maneuverability, and the high toe is a real asset in soft snow. This style is probably the most popular snowshoe in the West and is used throughout the U.S. snowbelt. Western snowshoes have their greatest advantage in soft but firm snow—as in the coastal mountains of the West and late winter snow elsewhere. Obviously, the smaller sizes will not provide adequate flotation in powder snow, except for light people.

An all-metal Western snowshoe, stamped from aluminum, is now on the market. Its edges are bent down all around, providing strength and excellent traction. The metal hinge is precise, with a quickly-adjusted snap-on binding and a spiked traction device attached to the bottom of the hinge and binding mechanism. However, this snowshoe is small for use on any but the firmest snow, and on hard crust it is noisy.

Another new development is plastic snowshoes. These have never been too well received in the mountains. Their greatest popularity has been for gentler hikes, for timber surveying, and for use as emergency equipment on snowmobiles. They are lightweight, priced lower than most others, and have a waxy surface that prevents snow from freezing or sticking to them as on wood and metal. They are flexible and the plastic used in some fatigues and breaks in time. But they are adequate for many hikes and the bright colors show up well in photos.

Characteristics

The basic shape of a snowshoe affects its handling characteristics. For example, the action of the snowshoe tail dragging on the snow and the toe rising in the air as the shoe is lifted is called tracking. A snowshoe with a long toe and a short, light tail does not track well; the toe often catches under deep snow or crust and must be wrenched free to prevent a fall. You should be able to simply lift each foot and shove it forward, knowing that the snowshoe will follow precisely. One 10×36-inch model with special forward-mounted toe cord tracks very well, in spite of its short length, as do the eight-inch-wide, short, aluminum-frame snowshoes.

Long Yukon 10×56-inch models track well, and their high toes seldom catch under the snow. Bearpaws do not track as well, and the toes often catch. Most short wood-frame snowshoes have such light tails that a relatively small weight of snow on the toe will cause it to catch, so that the tail rather than the toe rises as you step forward.

Beavertails seem to suffer from the same design weakness as the bearpaw: the toes are too long in relation to the tail. On level trails this tendency is not too noticeable, but when climbing, traversing, or descending, the wide, long toe section frequently runs under the snow and must be wrenched free to prevent a fall.

A snowshoe's traction is dependent on its webbing and cross bars biting into the snow, and some designs have better natural traction than others. The location of the toe cord in relation to the front of the snowshoe is vital. Placing the toe cord one-fourth of the length of the snowshoe from the toe improves traction by placing weight well forward, causing the toe to dig in deeper than on a snowshoe that supports weight nearer the tail. Figure 3 shows that the forward-mounted toe cord or binding hinge causes the snowshoe to almost make its own step as you climb a slope. On short snowshoes this has another advantage. The 10 × 36-inch standard snowshoe, for example, has such a long, nearly flat toe that it frequently catches, tripping the snowshoer (Figure 4). The forward toe cord changes the proportions of the 10 × 36-inch model so that the toe does not do this except possibly when descending. The weight of the tail section overbalances almost any load of snow the toe may gather when climbing.

Short, flat snowshoes with the forward toe cord do have this one weakness. When plunge-stepping—that is, taking long, stiff-kneed steps—downhill in soft snow, the toes dig in deeper than the tails. In this situation the toes can catch and cause a fall, especially if the snow is crusty. Using a snowshoe with a three- or four-inch turnup of the toe minimizes or eliminates the problem.

Even on easy snowshoe hikes there is a certain amount of scrambling over or around obstructions, which is neither climbing nor sidehilling. In the real backcountry this type of travel may predominate, with infrequent easy places. On such terrain a small, lightweight, maneuverable snowshoe with good tracking ability gives a real advantage.

The advantages of the 8 × 25 and 9 × 30 Western designs are their light weight, small size, ease of handling, and superb

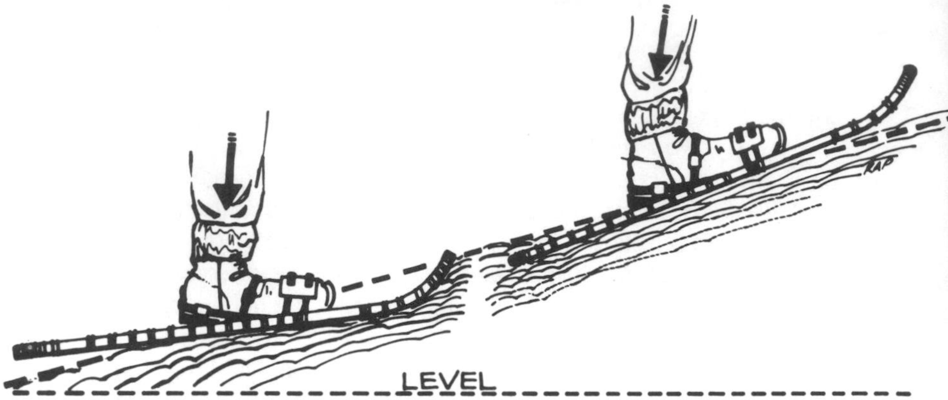

Fig. 3. Location of toe cord in relation to front of showshoe. Left is good—foot is forward, toe digs in, platform is more level, traction is good. Right is bad—foot is too far back, tail digs in, platform is steeply angled, traction is weak.

traction. Snowshoeing with these small snowshoes is an extension of the bare-boot walking or scrambling but on firm, hard snow. The small Western and 11 × 28 bearpaw make it possible to do this type of scrambling on snow too soft for bare-boot travel in much of the winter, though these snowshoes aren't practical for deep, loose new snow that hasn't firmed up.

It is possible for a snowshoe to sidehill and climb better than anyone else's, yet be so heavy and cumbersome that even a short hike is exhausting. Although the trend in snowshoes has

Fig. 4. Effect of length of toe. Left, short snowshoe with long toe catches under the snow easily; right, very short toe does not catch under the snow easily.

been toward small, narrow, lightweight models, some manufacturers still ignore this critical factor.

As the British planned their 1953 Mt. Everest expedition, it was calculated that one pound on the foot was as fatiguing as five pounds carried on the back, primarily because the distant end of the leg is an awkward and tiring place to carry extra weight. A 10 × 56-inch snowshoe with deluxe traction and binding weighs six to seven pounds. A small Western snowshoe weighs under two pounds. The extra eight pounds per pair of 10 × 56-inch snowshoes is the equivalent of 40 extra pounds in the pack.

Snowshoeing is tiring when compared to hiking in boots on a dry trail, and long, heavy snowshoes are exhausting unless you are conditioned to the extra weight. Small, light snowshoes, sufficient for support, will get you farther for equivalent effort.

Snowshoes may seem weightless compared to downhill skis, boots, and bindings. But when attempting to make turns on an uphill pull, it is a different story, especially for the lead person breaking trail through deep, heavy snow with its extra weight on the webs. And if you are on an overnight trip and have 40 or more pounds in your pack, you will appreciate the truth of the Everest formula.

Lacing

The traditional lacing material is raw, not tanned, cowhide. The heaviest available is necessary for mountain use. Two things put lacing to the test: moisture and abrasion. Rocks and other objects sticking through the snow, or thinly veiled by a layer of powder that hides but does not shield, can be a third, cutting the cord as the edges of chuck-holes do car tires.

Rawhide is the first choice for ability to survive abrasion and rock-cut damage in subfreezing temperatures. It is nearly indestructible as long as it stays cold. However, at temperatures above +30°F rawhide becomes soaked and loses about half its strength. When wet it stretches easily and loses much of its abrasion resistance.

Neoprene-covered nylon is the first choice for lacing snowshoes in wet snow, rating well above rawhide. Though wet spring snow above +30°F has sharp ice crystals that abrade both kinds of lace, neoprene lasts longer in such conditions than wet rawhide does. Neoprene also exceeds rawhide's ability to resist rock cuts at these temperatures.

Rock cuts may seem a minor hazard in the West, where there is supposed to be plenty of snow to cover such problems. But there are windswept ridges and plenty of downed conifers. Conifers have lots of branches and they seem to break with sharp ends. These sharp tips are certainly a hazard, especially in logged areas.

The East is where snowshoes take the worst beating in the North American snowbelt. The area near and above tree line is so wind-blasted that it usually seems to be more rock than snow. Trails are amazingly rocky, too, and steep sections—which are the majority of the trails—have granite clinkers the size of footballs covered with knife-pointed quartz crystals strewn liberally under a thin layer of powder snow. Choose heavy-duty lacing to snowshoe in this area.

The greatest weakness of neoprene lacing is probably quality control at the factory. When manufactured properly, the neoprene is firmly bonded to the nylon fiber that provides its strength. The nylon is very strong but wears out rapidly when rubbing on snow if the neoprene separates from it.

When buying, note whether the neoprene lacing appears "hairy" with lots of nylon fibers visible. Poor-quality neoprene shows here. After a season or two there may be so much nylon showing that it looks like rawhide with the hair left on and it will have lost much of its durability.

Neoprene-covered nylon abrades rapidly when wrapped around metal, faster than when wrapped around wood. Narrow quarter-inch-wide strips will likely fail quickly, especially at the tail of a round snowshoe, while one inch and wider nearer the front of the snowshoe will wear well.

Polyurethane is the newest lace material and was introduced in Western snowshoes. It rates above either rawhide or neoprene in abrasion resistance and like neoprene does not absorb water. It has great elasticity, which is one of its greatest assets. When under a strain it is more likely to stretch and spring back than to break either the lace or the frame.

Polyurethane ranks poorest of these three in resistance to cutting. Rocks knife through it because it contains no fiber, unlike neoprene lace; a nick may in time cause a break. Part of the problem is the metal frame, which the lace wraps around, because it is harder than wood. When the lace is pinched between a rock and the tubing, the lace may be severed. If you are going to snowshoe in an area with windswept, rocky ridges, look for the heaviest lace available.

Nylon cord is also used for lacing. It must be protected from abrasion since it does not survive rough crust or wet snow well. One West Coast manufacturer of Western snowshoes uses an epoxy coating on eighth-inch cord, and an eastern snowshoe maker has a varnish dip on quarter-inch rope. Again, the easterner may know more about snowshoeing on rocky ridges than the westerner.

The most visible difference between the Western snowshoe and the wood-frame snowshoe is the Western's synthetic decking, which takes the place of traditional webbing. Neoprene-covered nylon is the most common decking material, with various types of plastic or heavy upholstery fabric the other choices.

The waxy surface of the synthetic decking sheds snow better than the webbing does, permitting snow to slide off the snowshoe—an advantage when you're breaking trail. However, decking is extremely slippery, unlike webbing, which bites into the snow. As a result, all snowshoes with decking are equipped with a traction device.

Once in awhile someone compares decking with webbing and concludes that the webbing, with all those openings, provides less flotation than the decking. However, snow doesn't slide through small openings well at all. In a laboratory situation with precise test equipment, a difference might be detected, but on the trail, any difference in flotation is imperceptible to even the fussiest snowshoer.

Choosing a Snowshoe

Frame design, webbing or decking, tracking, toe turnup, size, and weight all affect choice of snowshoe. Every design has some disadvantages. A compromise must be made when buying, because no design solves all problems for all people in all places. And sometimes people as independently minded as snowshoers pick their snowshoe because they like a certain shape or material, although we "experts" recommend something else. If you want to go snowshoeing somewhere, almost any kind will get you there if you are determined enough.

Most areas have a local tradition for choosing snowshoes.

The variety of sizes and shapes with light or heavy lacing still available from Canadian manufacturers is nearly overwhelming, but few shops in the United States have a large choice of models and sizes. Although I haven't snowshoed in every snowy area in North America, I have some suggestions to help a beginner.

Different geographical areas have quite different requirements for snowshoes. For example, in the western coastal ranges where "warm" winter temperatures cause the snow to firm up quickly, small Western snowshoes work very well. Often a 200-pound person will be quite happy with the smallest size, although most people prefer more flotation.

The interior of British Columbia; the Rockies of Montana, Wyoming, and Colorado; the Wasatch of Utah; and the Sierra of California are a great deal colder than the Cascades of Washington and Oregon. Snow is fluffier, so a larger snowshoe is required for flotation.

Wherever you snowshoe, you will hear of some person who traveled great distances on immense snowshoes while sinking knee-deep—or more—in bottomless powder snow. Any of the mountain areas mentioned can have 24 to 36 inches or more of snowfall overnight, and 8 to 10 feet or more if the storm lasts several days. Few recreational snowshoers travel very far under such conditions, unless they were caught back in the hills by the storm and must get out in a given time. Old-timers have a tendency to sneer at present-day short, narrow, lightweight snowshoes that obviously will sink out of sight in the fluff deposited by such a storm. It takes a snowshoe like a 12 × 62-inch Yukon or 19 × 26-inch bearpaw to travel in really soft snow. Actually, this kind of major storm is rather infrequent. The old tradition of iron men on big snowshoes is being put to rest. It is less exhausting to wait a few days for new snow to firm up and then use smaller lightweight equipment. It also is safer in avalanche country to wait a few days and let the slides run, too.

If you are carrying a heavy pack and sinking 12 inches in powder snow on giant snowshoes, you may travel only a few miles in rough country in a hard day. Sinking in 18 inches or more, which is about knee-deep, you may measure the distance traveled in yards rather than miles. So especially in mountain country snowshoers are waiting for firm snow and replacing their large heavy snowshoes with smaller lightweight models.

Snow travel is so much easier on firm snow than on the bottomless variety that waiting a few days is well worth it.

A snowshoer in Anchorage, Alaska, prefers a 9×38-inch Western for local outings, although in some winters of cold weather and exceptionally heavy snowfall a larger snowshoe would be better. The same size, 9×38 or 10×36 Western, will also be adequate for mountain country in interior British Columbia, Montana, and Wyoming.

For the northern Rockies of Colorado, one snowshoer suggests a 9×30-inch Western as large enough for the snow. This size or 9×38 will probably be a good choice here or in the Wasatch and Sierra. Routes are possible near and above timber line that are wind-packed and also exposed to the bright late-winter sun, which speeds firming the snow.

A mountain guide who climbs in the Purcells in winter advises that if you can't kick steps with your snowshoe, it's no good in the mountains. This is good advice, and if the snowshoe is over three feet long, it's too unwieldy for mountain use.

Easterners agree. However, step kicking in the eastern mountains is probably more severe than in any other area of North America. Typically, there is a crust on the snow there. Snowshoes must have nearly flat toes and are really bashed into the crust to make a step.

This technique may leave most of the snowshoe sticking out in the air, whereas in soft western snow—either wet and sloppy or powder—the snowshoe is rather casually stomped down to make a deep step with only the tail sticking out. The difference in surfaces has led to two very different styles of kicking steps and different snowshoes best adapted to these techniques. As one is definitely East and the other West, I use the terms eastern technique and western technique.

There are many more Western snowshoes with high toes—three to six inches of turnup—in use in the coastal mountains of the West than there are flat beavertails and bearpaws. The Western snowshoe is also becoming a popular choice in New England, too, although there are lots of wood snowshoes still used in this area.

Comfort on descents also has a bearing on whether to choose flat or high toes. Most western mountains have soft snow throughout the winter, seldom crusting as the eastern mountains do after a January thaw. So descents are generally in soft snow, where a high toe helps keep the snowshoe from run-

A steep pitch en route to the summit of Cannon Mountain, New Hampshire

ning under the snow and tripping the snowshoer.

In addition to easterners, another category of snowshoers usually puts climbing ability as the highest priority for snowshoe choice after deciding what size is needed. These are people who work on steep, timbered slopes in winter surveying or in marking trees for logging. Climbing usually involves kicking steps, so their first choice is often a low or flat toe. Timber surveyors often follow compass lines, section lines, or other routes that must be followed as precisely as possible no matter how rugged the terrain is. Deep gullies must be crossed and steep hills ascended while pulling a 100-foot or longer tape to get accurate measure; it isn't permitted to detour around even one tree just because there's an easier way on the other side. So if you can't get up the slope on the chosen line with poor climbing snowshoes, there's no need to be concerned about the descent.

The emphasis so far has been on snowshoes for mountain country. The problems created by steep slopes and hard snow are best solved by fairly small snowshoes that can be placed very accurately just where you want them. For more gentle terrain, the main concern is to have enough flotation without excessive weight. The larger the snowshoe, the less you sink in soft snow. The shape may be long and narrow or short and wide.

One way to see for yourself which snowshoe has the larger surface (and thus more flotation) is to place one on top of another and estimate how much bigger it is. Three snowshoes with nearly the same supporting surface are in the Yukon and bearpaw categories. The 10×56-inch and 10×46-inch Yukons and 10×36-inch Green Mountain, a bearpaw-style snowshoe with a rounded tail, don't have as much difference as the dimensions would lead you to expect. The 10×56-inch is 20 inches longer than the 10×36-inch, but most of the difference is in the long, skinny tail and the high toe, which don't add much flotation.

A second comparison to make is between the size of the snowshoer and the snowshoe itself. Avoid putting a five-foot-long snowshoe on a very short person. A strapping six-foot, four-inch athlete can make a lot of mileage on large, heavy snowshoes without excessive fatigue. Tiny women, middle-aged sedentary persons, and young teenagers probably don't have the stamina to do this. Match a person's dimensions to the snowshoe.

Also keep in mind that a wide snowshoe forces a person to walk with the feet wide apart (Figure 5). To hold the feet apart so a wide snowshoe doesn't bump you on the opposite ankle or calf is tiring to the tendons on the outside of each hip joint. A first-time snowshoer on wide, heavy snowshoes is often surprised at the new pain from this exertion, locally termed "ball joint fatigue."

Choose a snowshoe that will work well in a variety of conditions. In general all through the snowbelt, you will find the softest, deepest powder snow in December and January. In February it will be firming up. March and April will find firm snow. Heavy snowfalls in late winter firm up faster than in January. The farther north you are, the later these stages occur. However, I was rained on in the Cascades of Washington, the White Mountains of New Hampshire, and the Purcells of British Columbia in January and February of 1979. Winter weather is so capricious that there may be a lot more variety in snow conditions than you expected.

I've used a great many sizes and shapes of snowshoes, on various terrains and types of snow. Over the years I've experimented with lots of gimmicks as well as accepted designs and have ended up handcrafting my own snowshoes. For powder snow in early winter I use a 7½ × 40-inch Western-type snowshoe. For firm snow, such as late winter in the Cascades and spring in colder ranges, a 7½ × 30-inch design is adequate. There are times when it is less fatiguing to sink a little deeper with a small snowshoe that handles easily than fight a big, heavy snowshoe.

If the route doesn't climb steeply and the snow is exceedingly deep and soft, my first choice is an 11 × 57-inch Cree rawhide-laced wood snowshoe with pointed toe and tail. Toe upturn is five to six inches. (The Cree is a Yukon design but has a distinctive two-piece frame with a pointed toe.)

For descending steep slopes in this same deep powder, a 12 × 62-inch or 10 × 56-inch Yukon with six-inch turnup is unbeatable. Unfortunately, these don't climb steep slopes well. A 19 × 26-inch bearpaw has the most flotation of any snowshoe I've used. It is good for kicking steps straight up with its short, flat toe, and good for descending because the tails can be kicked in well in either powder or crust. It is impossible to

Fig. 5. Walking with spraddled stance while carrying extra weight places distinctive strain on hip tendons.

traverse steep sidehills since each snowshoe is more than twice as wide as Western snowshoes. They are heavy as well as wide and are exhausting to wear.

I've waded through streams in 25°F temperatures and out onto powder snow with plastic snowshoes without the problem of chipping frozen slush off them. The waxy surface prevented this. A fiberglass snowshoe I used a couple of times is very strong and a fairly good design for mountains. I used them on a warm day with wet, sloppy snow, yet none stuck to the fiberglass, although laced snowshoes became wet and heavy with some snow packed against the lacing under the boot. The re-

Snowshoe Guidelines

	FLAT TERRAIN		MOUNTAINS		
Weight	**Powder**	**Firm**	**Powder**	**Firm**	**New England**
175 pounds and up	Minimum Size 10 × 46 Yukon 10 × 36 Modified Bearpaw 9 × 38 Western 15 × 33 Bearpaw 14 × 42 Beavertail	9 × 30 Western 10 × 36 Modified Bearpaw 12 × 34 Beavertail 8 × 25 Western 9 × 30 Western	10 × 36 Modified Bearpaw 11 × 35 Beavertail	9 × 30 Western 9 × 38 Western 10 × 36 Modified Bearpaw 8 × 25 Western 9 × 30 Western	12 × 34 Beavertail 12 × 28 Bearpaw
150–175	Same as above	8 × 25 Western 9 × 30 Western 9 × 30 Western 12 × 28 Bearpaw 12 × 34 Beavertail	Same as above	9 × 30 Western 8 × 25 Western 12 × 28 Bearpaw 12 × 34 Beavertail	Same as above
Under 150	Same plus 9 × 30 Western 12 × 28 Bearpaw 12 × 34 Beavertail	Same as above	Same plus 8 × 25 Western	Same as above	Same as above

turn was after sundown and the chill of evening quickly put a frozen crust on the snow. The fiberglass was quite resonant as the crust cracked underfoot, and conversation was impossible. It sounded like I was walking on a cement sidewalk with a metal garbage-can lid on each foot.

For gentle country, the 11- or 12-inch-wide by 36- to 44-inch-long beavertail has long been number one. And whether it's level country or mountain, I'd rather be patient and wait for good traveling conditions so I can use a small, lightweight snowshoe instead of the large ones listed above. These are reasonable compromises. If you are going snowshoeing in gentle country, you don't need all that heavy equipment designed for mountains.

Most manufacturers rate their snowshoes for weight of person and type of snow. An old, simplified pre-Western snowshoe suggestion of mine is as follows: 200 pounds and over rates a 10 × 56-inch Yukon or equivalent; 175–200 pounds does well on a 10 × 46-inch Yukon design; 150–175 pounds moves easily on 10 × 36-inch modified bearpaw or 12 × 34-inch beavertail. Those weighing under 150 pounds can easily wear 12 × 28-inch bearpaw or 10 × 33-inch beavertail. The table on page 26 includes a broader listing of type of terrain and snow and regional preferences. When picking your weight range, don't forget to allow for heavy pack.

Maintenance and Repair

Wood frames and rawhide need routine maintenance. Clear spar varnish or shellac is the traditional material, although some people prefer more color, and paint is nearly as durable as varnish. Whenever the finish wears off the wood, it's time to get out the brush and redo the snowshoe. The same rule of thumb applies to the rawhide. Powder snow is not very abrasive and in cold temperatures there is very littler wear on the bottoms of the snowshoes. In wet snow the story is different, since rawhide soon begins to get soaked and varnish starts flaking off. Most of us have seen snowshoes with the rawhide bleached out and wear showing on the frames. The hard part of the wood grain stands out, because softer wood fibers have been worn away.

A special Cascade Mountain recipe for early-1900s "Snowshoe Dope" comes from Morris Jenkins of Cle Elum,

Washington, who trapped and cruised timber for years on snowshoes. The special ingredient is pitch from a fir tree. This must be of thin-syrup consistency and can come from two sources. One is an old-growth tree with a "wind-shook" seam, where a living tree has a split that is still dripping pitch after it has been felled during logging. Sometimes a gallon may be collected from one tree of this type. The second source is pitch blisters on a growing tree, but this is a lot messier job and takes much longer to collect.

For those of you who actually have access to either such tree, the dope is eight parts clear shellac, two parts pitch, and one part beeswax (paraffin). Heat and mix thoroughly, but do not boil. Warm the snowshoe to room temperature. Use a small paintbrush and paint the frames, lacing, and binding with the dope. This will waterproof and protect even in wet snow since it doesn't dry brittle but stays flexible. Two dopings per winter should be sufficient for heavy use in coastal slush; however, more applications may be necessary if wear takes off the earlier coating. Do not dry a snowshoe near a hot fire because it can damage rawhide, neoprene, polyurethane, and wood frames.

Neoprene lace is a no-maintenance material, but if it gets "hairy," as described earlier, it may be a good idea to give it a haircut. Some jogging shoe repair cement will prolong life if the lacing gets worn under your boot heel—a place of considerable abrasion—or where a rock has snagged it so the nylon fibers show.

The metal-frame and synthetic-decking snowshoes are advertised as no-maintenance. This is fairly accurate. However, the need to varnish wood snowshoes made it imperative to examine them minutely several times each winter. This way you picked up any nearly broken webbing or other problems. Check over no-maintenance "webs" periodically. It's better to find and repair problems at home, where tools are available and the work can be done at a comfortable temperature. It can be almost overwhelming to discover that your snowshoes are falling apart after dark in a blizzard when it's still several miles back to the car.

The variety of slopes and snow conditions in hill or mountain country tends to present situations that are harder on snowshoes than those presented by open country. The main cause of a broken frame is stepping on a hole or depression in such a way that the toe and tail of the shoe are on higher points than the middle of the foot, with perhaps the middle 24 inches of the frame bridging the hole. Often ridgetops are blown free of snow, revealing sharp rocks and frozen clods that cut webbing and damage frames. There are many obstructions lightly covered by snow, such as fallen trees, branches, and rocks. A gentle step may do no more than scratch the frame, but jumping off something may create enough force to break the frame or cut the webbing. (Snowshoers seem to delight in jumping off things because the soft landing is so different from crashing down on bare ground.) But stepping into small depressions; jumping onto hard, hummocky snow; wading rocky streambeds; and falling into tree holes are the most common damaging maneuvers.

First aid for a broken frame is the same as for a broken bone. In forested country, cut a couple of small branches to use as splints; lay one on top and one under the break, and wrap tightly with eighth-inch nylon cord (Figure 6). This will last quite well, especially since the snowshoer will then be much more careful of the footgear.

Incidentally, frame breakage has not been a problem with metal frames. However, any frame that is accidentally bent while snowshoeing will break completely if straightened. An emergency field repair is the same splint used to repair a broken wooden snowshoe. Carry plenty of eighth-inch nylon cord for repairs, no matter what kind of snowshoe you are using. And hope there is a convenient branch to provide the splint.

Broken rawhide and neoprene webbing are spliced the same way (Figure 7). Make a lengthwise split in the ends, thread the repair cord through, tighten, and tie off. It is hard to do a neat job of this with either the blade or the leather punch of your knife without a lot of practice. It is easy, however, to cut slices in straps and laces when the knife slips, and with the same stroke slice through good webbing and end up with the point of the knife stuck in your hand. To prevent this "great downward slash," place the webbing or strap on the frame of your wood snowshoe—or on any available stick—press down firmly, and use several strokes of your recently sharpened knife to make the cut. Wet rawhide is exceedingly slimy and snaky and has a tendency to roll over when you are making the cuts.

Repair of a cut polyurethane lace is difficult in the field and happens too seldom to suggest that the clips and pliers

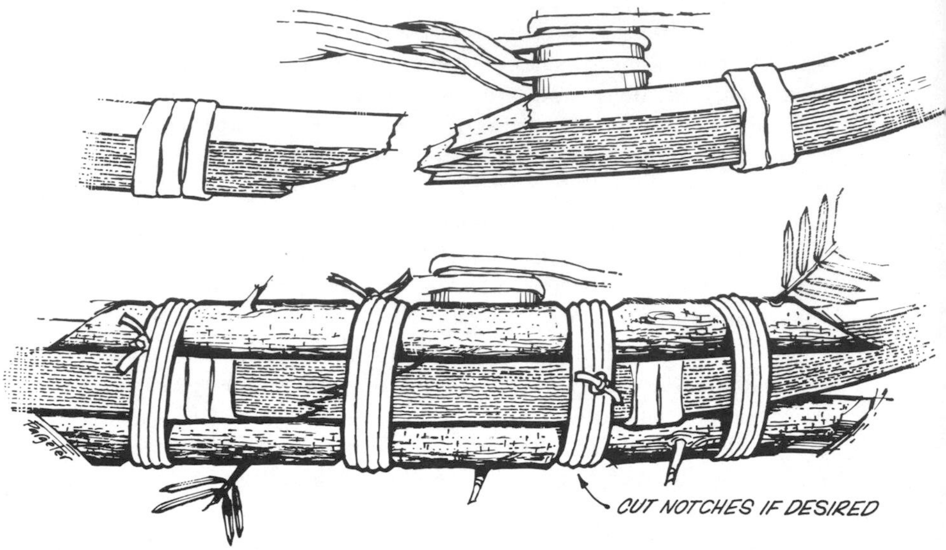

Fig. 6. Repairing a broken frame with a splint of branches. Four wraps of cord will hold it in place.

Fig. 7. Splice for broken strap or webbing. Cut slit in ends near break, thread cord through, pull tight and tie.

used by the manufacturer be carried in one's repair kit. It is practically impossible to tie anything to this slippery, flexible material. However, unrepaired lace can unravel along quite a length of snowshoe. Carry nylon cord or plastic heavy-duty electrical-wire ties to hold things together until back home, where more permanent repairs can be made.

For broken nylon cord it's best to tie loops in the broken ends, thread repair cord through these loops, and tie off. Knots in nylon have a tendency to come untied unless you really tighten them down—and even then you can't trust them.

I use the word Western as a design or type, as these snowshoes are so different from wood-frame laced models. Twenty years ago the first Western snowshoe to be sold throughout the snow belt was manufactured in Washington state. At present the name doesn't fit geographically. The original Western is still made in California. The former Washington Western is now sold from Chicago. A recent Western calls Colorado home. The newest Westerns are made in Vermont and California. A wood snowshoe maker in New York makes wood-frame laced Westerns. My few pairs of handmade Westerns are still made in Washington.

Although most present equipment is far superior to what was available in 1950, and the limits of snowshoes on slopes have been expanded dramatically, there are still many possibilities for improvement. Someday someone is going to get it all together, and then today's "modern" equipment will be comparable to the *Spirit of St. Louis,* hanging in the Smithsonian, as jet aircraft flit by overhead.

Snowshoeing off the summit of Telescope Peak, above California's Death Valley, in distance

CHAPTER 2

Bindings

The second vital part of the basic snowshoe package is the binding, which must make a positive connection between the foot and the snowshoe. To allow comfortable walking, the binding must hinge freely, the heel rising as the boot toe goes into the toe hole (Figure 8). Any restriction on the hinging movement will limit a comfortable stride. If the binding or boot hits the side of the toe hole or catches on the toe bar, it may cause the snowshoe toe to dig in and trip the wearer. The binding should be easily adjustable so that any such problems can be quickly remedied.

The binding should strictly limit the hinging action to up and down motion, gripping the boot tightly so there is practically no lateral movement. When the foot turns left or right, the snowshoe should turn precisely the same way, with preferably less than an inch of sideways movement at the boot heel on wood snowshoes and no such lateral movement on Westerns (the precise binding hinge prevents it). When the snowshoe responds this positively, it is possible to move confidently through rough terrain without tripping on obstacles or slipping on sidehills.

Fig. 8. Binding should hinge freely up and down, with toe of boot fitting through toe hole in snowshoe.

Binding Adjustment

The binding must grip the boot firmly to keep it from slipping forward, particularly when descending. If the boot slides forward, the heel strap can drop off the heel and let the boot slip backwards out of the binding on the next step, or the boot toe will ride up on the toe bar, depressing the toe of the snowshoe and causing it to catch. No matter what kind of bindings you have, you need to know the basics of how to adjust them.

Incidentally, a broken binding strap can be repaired by joining the two ends with cord as described in chapter 1, or without repair cord by splicing the separated end through the splits as shown in Figure 9.

Expertise at tightening the bindings while standing on the snowshoe must be developed. To check for slack in the binding-to-snowshoe attachment, wiggle the binding side to side before strapping them to your boots. This is the time—before you are on the trail—to do the adjusting. No matter how firmly the binding is buckled to the boot it will not work properly if there is slack in the attachment to the snowshoe. The

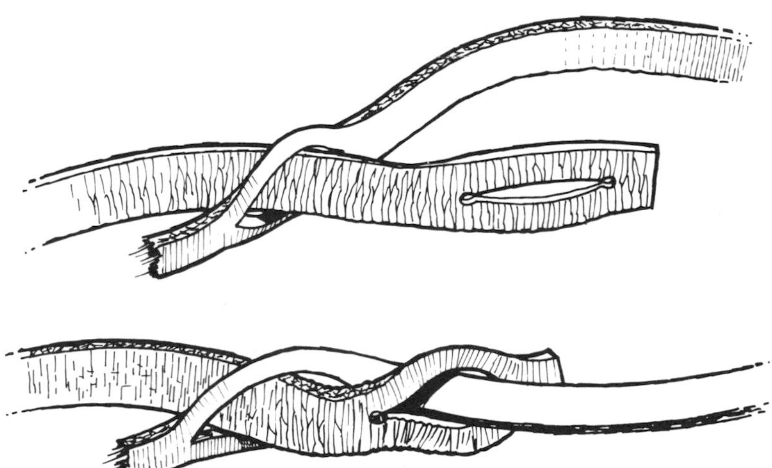

Fig. 9. Splicing a broken strap. First slip split end of severed section (top) onto other piece. Then slip loose end of severed section through hole in end of other piece, and pull tight.

binding must be kept tight on the toe cord or binding hinge of the snowshoe. Straps wear and stretch, periodically developing slack. Work the slack out of the straps that hold the binding to the toe cord before you strap on the boots. On some models thongs must be tightened; on some the slack in the heel strap is pulled through the leather of the binding.

Types of Bindings

Figure 10 is an improved H binding, which is one of the most popular bindings. The boot is held firmly but may come out of the binding if you fall forward. The boot toe can slip back from under the toe strap, or on a steep sidehill, the boot heel may rotate sideways to allow the boot to slip from under the toe strap.

It takes some doing to put these on your snowshoes the first time, so make sure a diagram comes with the bindings if you buy them separate from the snowshoes. Once the binding is on the snowshoe, slip your boot into it, with straps unbuckled, so the ball of the foot is just behind or on the snowshoe toe cord. Center your boot in the toe hole so that it doesn't touch lacing on either side. Lift the heel and make sure the boot toe doesn't touch the toe bar. Tighten the toe strap firmly on the boot toe, then the heel strap, and last the instep strap. All buckles should be on the outside of your boot so strap ends won't catch on the other snowshoe and trip you. Recheck soon after you start your hike. If your boot toe catches on the toe bar when going downhill, loosen heel strap, slide boot back, tighten toe strap to prevent this, and retighten other straps.

To remove your snowshoes, unbuckle heel and instep straps and slide boot out. If the same boot is used each time, the toe strap adjustment can be left. Set up this way, the H binding is the fastest to put on and take off. All adjustments can be made with mittens on, if the straps are long enough.

Several bindings similar to the improved H are available. However, one such binding, the standard H, does not have the toe piece that traps the boot toe and prevents it from sliding forward to catch on the toe bar. This toe piece is probably most useful on soft-toe shoe pacs rather than hard-toe climbing boots because it is painful to tighten the toe strap down really tight on your toes in soft footgear. On level or gentle terrain there is little problem with the boot sliding forward out of the

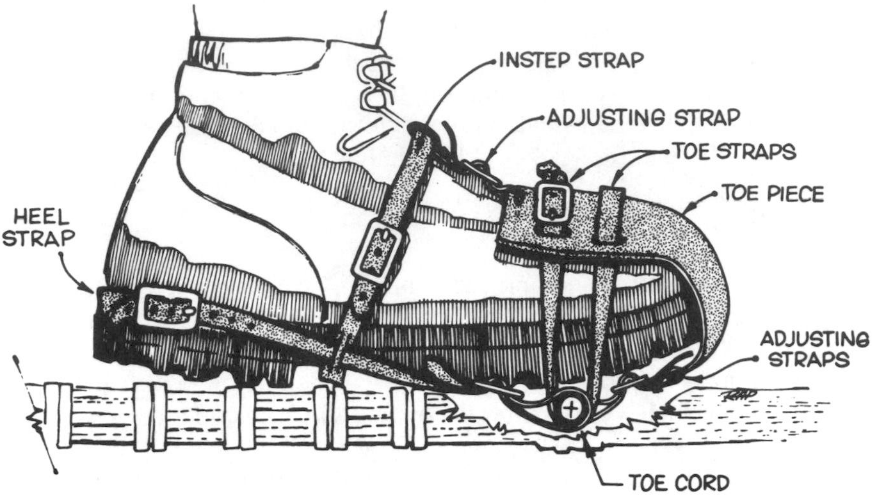

Fig. 10. Improved H binding

binding anyway; this is chiefly a problem when descending steep mountain slopes.

There is a limit to how tight the toe strap may be tightened. It must slide around the toe cord to allow the hinging action. If it is so tight that the tail of the snowshoe rises off the

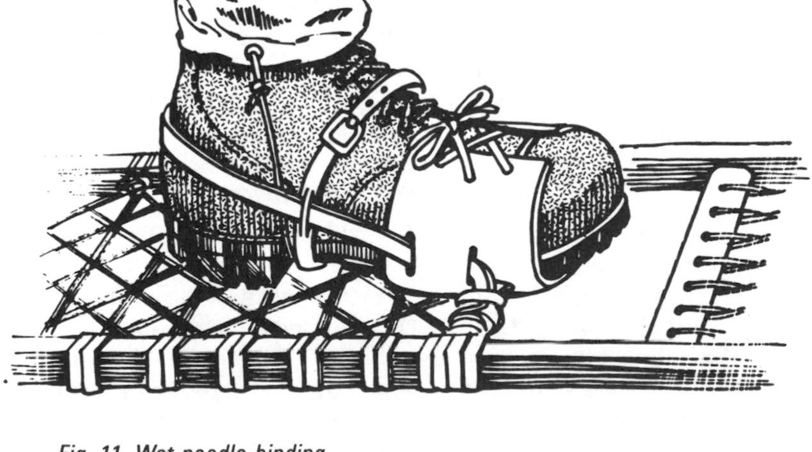

Fig. 11. Wet noodle binding

snow each step, better loosen the toe strap or check the instruction sheet to be sure the binding is mounted correctly.

The wet noodle binding (Figure 11) is, like the H binding, an old standby that is available at most shops all across the snowbelt. Most people adjust it the same as the H, tying the lace in one place and unbuckling the heel strap to take them off. There is not really any good way to keep the boot from sliding forward on steep descents, so this binding is better for gentle terrain.

The Western binding design (Figure 12) has been proven in the field since the 1950s and is an improvement on previous binding designs. Western snowshoes come equipped with the binding shown or with a similar one. Western bindings are available for use on wood snowshoes, too. They are attached to the master cord with straps similar to the wet noodle binding (Figure 12). Actually, the wet noodle binding shown here was the binding that evolved into the original Western. The solid-fabric body was enlarged and stronger material used, and the holes were replaced with hooks and D rings and the thong with a strap and buckle. The binding fits most sizes of boots and works well on both soft boots such as pacs, with rubber lowers and leather uppers, and even better on leather or plastic climbing boots.

The most secure method of tightening the Western binding onto your boot follows. Place the boot in the binding with the boot toe protruding through the binding about one inch. Then tighten the heel strap so the boot can't slip backwards. Place the heel strap in the groove between sole and upper; if there isn't a groove, move the strap up to the Achilles tendon area, two to three inches above the boot heel (Figure 13).

Now tighten the toe strap through the hooks or D rings, at the same time pulling the boot firmly back against the heel strap. A tighter adjustment is possible if you raise the boot heel and wiggle it against the heel strap while pulling with both hands on the generous toe strap. Keep the boot heel centered on the snowshoe. Most Western bindings have buckles with spring-loaded latches, which automatically grip the strap and hold the adjustment (an occasional buckle does not and should be replaced). To loosen the strap, hold the latch open with a finger and pull the strap back out.

Some newer models of Western bindings have a fabric extension that has a hook at its end and is located at the front of

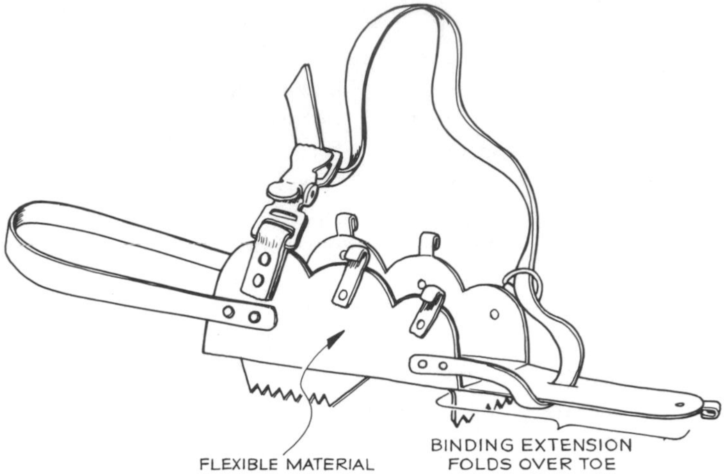

Fig. 12. Western binding with extension

the binding. You fold the extension over the boot toe before you begin to tighten the toe strap. After you have tightened the strap around the second or third set of hooks from the binding's front, you pull the strap around the extension's hook.

The purpose of this extension is to correct the most an-

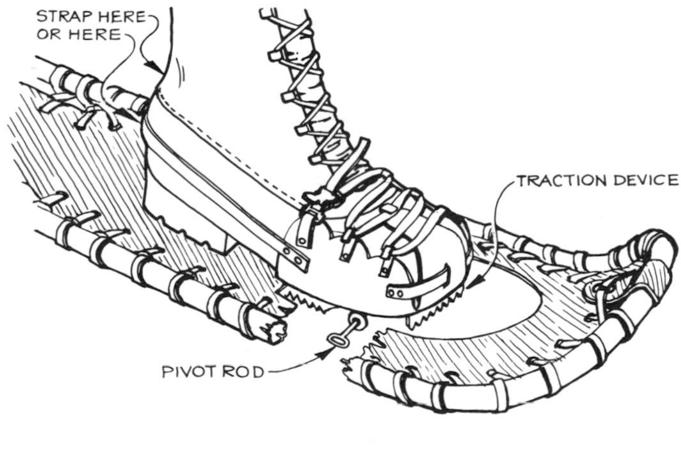

Fig. 13. Western binding with extension attached to snowshoe

noying problem common to all bindings: as you descend, your boot works so far forward that the heel strap drops off and you walk out of the binding. The next step is surprisingly deep.

When this happens, retrieve the snowshoe, knock the snow off your boot, and put the snowshoe back on, this time getting the toe strap tight enough, and all the slack out of the heel strap as well, to minimize the problem.

Snowshoers frequently set their boots as far forward in the bindings as they can without catching their boot toes on the front decking or crosspiece. The purpose is to stick the boot toe as far down as possible into the snow when they take a step, increasing their traction in steep places. This can be an advantage in climbing, but the benefit is offset somewhat because the boot slides forward when they descend, increasing their chance of walking out of the bindings. No firm rule of thumb need be dreamed up here. Snowshoe performance is increased by making small compromises. Those who put their boot toes as far forward in their bindings as possible probably have the point of view that if you can't get up it, your snowshoes won't fall off your boots coming back down it! With experience and some careful study, you will become more proficient at putting your snowshoes on in the morning so that they will need no additional tightening or adjusting until you take them off in the evening.

Several styles of Western bindings are sold for use on wood snowshoes. These can be an improvement over the H and other traditional bindings, but they have one requirement to be aware of: the toe hole of the snowshoe must be at least 4½ inches wide. Be sure your wood snowshoes are compatible with Western bindings before purchasing a set.

Few wood snowshoes are sold equipped with bindings, in contrast to Western snowshoes. Most wood snowshoes have a standard toe-hole dimension and accept several designs of bindings. There are Canadian snowshoes, particularly racing models, that do not have the rectangular toe hole and are designed for the lampwick binding (Figure 14).

The lampwick and squaw hitch bindings are virtually unknown outside eastern Canada and New England, where the lampwick is used for snowshoe races. It can be a good emergency binding, and when properly tightened to the boot it will hold well and hinge excellently. It is used in races from 60 yards to 10 miles, including hurdles.

Fig. 14. Canadian racing snowshoe with Lampwick binding

A large part of the snowshoeing public can overlook much of what I've written about bindings for rugged snowshoeing. Plenty of people enjoy a level hike and aren't traveling very many miles. It's possible to get inexpensive, lightweight snowshoes with simple bindings and lightweight shoe pacs and be quite a few dollars—not mention pounds on the foot—ahead.

When you're not in mountain country with a bunch of tigers trying to bag a couple of peaks before the next storm strikes, you don't have to have all that fancy geetus—that's east slope Cascade language for gear. You will have time to stop and tighten a binding, put a patch on a blister, and share the beauty of the place you're at with your companions.

But if you are in tough country, the best is none too good. If you're in top shape, with a fast party, and conditions are really great and there's a special viewpoint just about half an hour ahead, it's distressing to be floundering and falling due to a loose or poorly fitted binding. It's fatiguing to be fussing with your gear when a first-time snowshoer is walking effortlessly past because that person got first-rate equipment and everything is working just right.

Actually, the purpose of being out there is to see, smell, and experience the beauty of winter, not to study the deficiencies of some old ragtag snowshoe bindings.

CHAPTER 3

Traction Devices and Balance Aids

A real landmark for the two of us who purchased Yukons in December 1950 was a four-day trip up Ingalls Creek to Mt. Stuart, the 9415-foot peak dominating central Washington's mountains. Conditions for snowshoeing were good, with the exception of the icy depressions under each tree where the drip of melting snow off the branches had refrozen. Our new "guaranteed-not-to-sag" snowshoes didn't bite into the ice at all and we slipped considerably, but quick sprints created enough momentum to effectively cross these minor difficulties. Early in the trip, however, it was obvious that one section of hard snow would be sufficient to seriously hamper progress up the trail.

Also in the area was a trapper, whose boot imprint, with criss-cross webbing under it, showed clearly in each snowshoe track. His rawhide webbing sagged badly but provided excellent, if temporary, traction in the process. This certainly wasn't a satisfactory solution, as sagging rawhide soon breaks, but it did indicate that a small area that could bite into hard snow prevented the slipping and sliding we were experiencing.

Other snowshoers and I began a lengthy trial-and-error process of bolting, lacing, and tying different types of rough and sharp-edged objects so they would protrude below the bottom of the wood snowshoe and bite into hard snow (Figure 15). We tried attaching small pieces of aluminum angles to the frames at different curves and angles, wrapping rope and rawhide around the frames, and adding knotted rope to the webbing under the boot. Although these modifications helped, they were not enough.

The aluminum angles worked effectively except for one problem: walking is more comfortable and efficient if the foot, and especially the ball of the foot, can be placed directly on top of any slightly higher point in a trail for the greatest traction. A traction angle attached to the toe bar is about six inches in front of the ball of the foot and must be placed where it will get the best grip. In places with tricky footing—crossing a stream on icy stepping stones or a slippery foot log—it was obvious that the traction should be directly under the foot so that the entire body weight would force the device to bite into the ice or hard crust. Not only did this new positioning of the traction prove more comfortable and efficient, it was thus possible to use a smaller and lighter device than one placed on the toe bar or frame. The traction must be effective in all directions so it will hold when going straight up or down, traversing, or angling uphill. A single

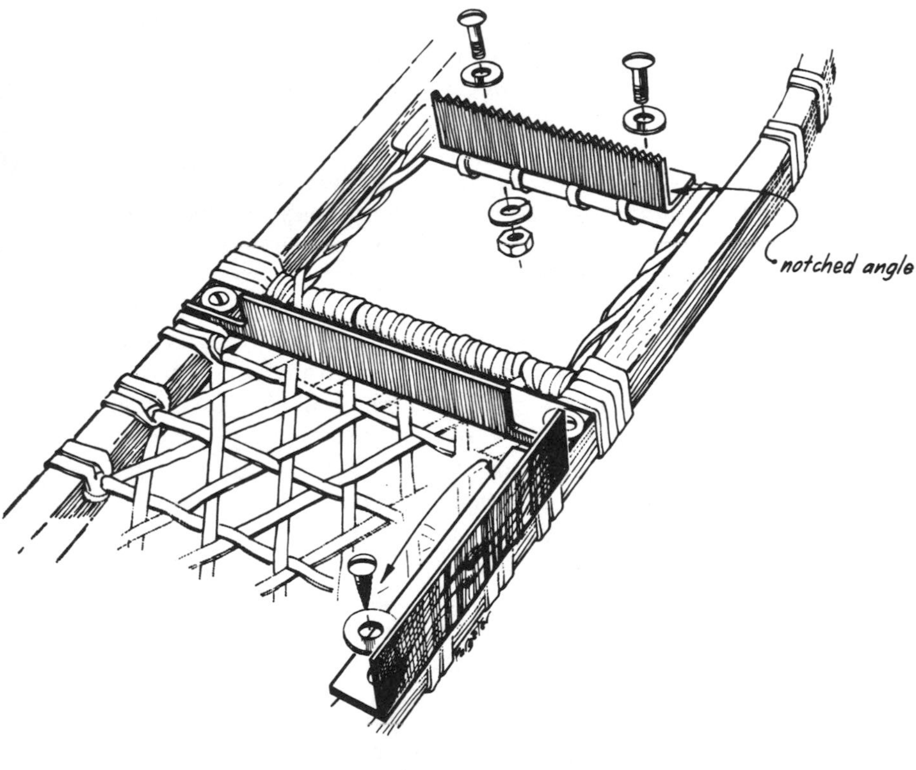

Fig. 15. Traditional home workshop traction devices installed on bottom of frame and toe bar. Not all of these pieces are necessary at once.

smooth, straight bar is useless when sidehilling; on a hard crust it will act like a sled runner, speeding you on your way.

Snowshoers in the East also arrived at a solution to the traction problem. The toughest conditions for snowshoeing are normal in their mountain areas. Cold temperatures create acres of ice on rock slabs and each seep of water in a trail freezes into yards of ice by New Year's. Trails in this area don't subscribe to the switchback ethic, and there are miles of trail that go straight up steep hills with a thicket of stunted trees on either side—locally known as Krummholz—that can't be penetrated on snowshoes. The ground above tree line is often not as steep, and summits and ridges are rounded, but generally the area is sheathed in rime ice, an ice crust that forms when clouds cover the area above treeline in subfreezing weather. The January thaw warms things up briefly before subzero temperatures clamp down again, putting a crust on snow from valley floor to tree line.

So an instep crampon lashed to the snowshoe webbing directly under the binding is required equipment. No serrated or smooth angle aluminum is sufficient to dent the case-hardened crust on these low-elevation, but quite formidable, mountains. The inch-long five or six steel points on the crampon are superb for the trail problems of ice and crust and the equal of most other traction devices in soft snow. However, above tree line and on slides, boot crampons normally replace snowshoes.

At least one U.S. supplier stocks instep crampons, which are not hard to install on laced snowshoes. The parts that hold the rings for strapping to your boots can be broken off easily by bending them down with pliers or a pry bar. Figure 16 shows a simple job of lashing the crampons to the snowshoe webbing. Most of these crampons are tempered carbon steel, so it is not possible to bore holes in them.

The most popular Western snowshoe has a shallow, serrated three-sided traction device or claw, or a spike crampon arrangement factory-made as an integral part of the metal hinge (Figure 17). This is a most satisfactory unit, and its combination with the Western binding also available gives excellent control of the snowshoe. For soft snow and moderate crust this product is quite adequate and something I'd have given an arm for back in 1950 when sliding and crashing in the icy tree holes on that first memorable outing.

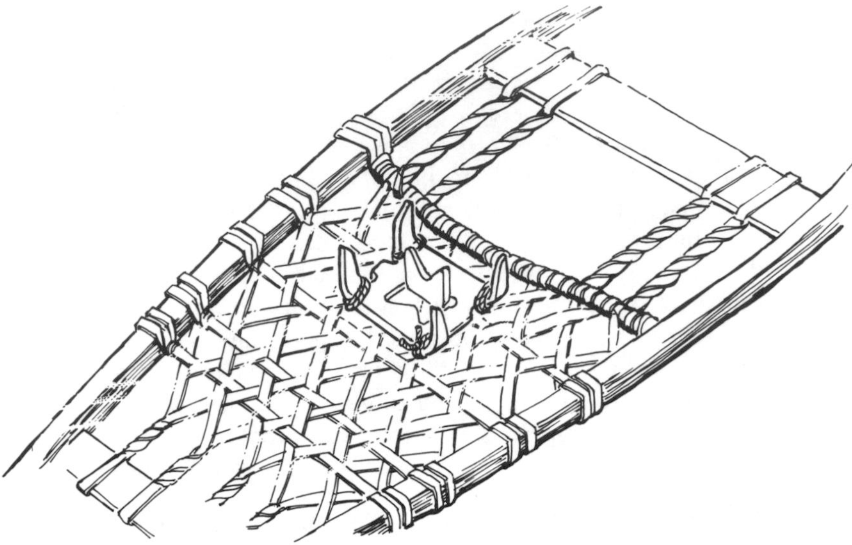

Fig. 16. Crampon lashed to laced snowshoe

Other Western snowshoes have a serrated angle the width of the snowshoe. This serves as the front crosspiece or is attached to the crosspiece, putting it directly under the ball of the foot, where it is nearly as effective as the three-sided traction described above. The serrated angle does not provide lateral grip, although on snowshoes with an angle frame, this is not a problem.

It is obvious that the present traction devices are among the greatest aids to snowshoeing on varied terrain. The unmodified snowshoe performs comfortably on a very low limit of slope, and there seems to be a steep or icy spot on every trip, regardless of how short or easy it is supposed to be. Tensed up, edging the snowshoes mightily, bent forward from the waist with hands extended to catch yourself when—not if—you slip, you will soon be too tired to proceed. The energy drain from tension is tremendous. It is acceptable to be tired after covering a lot of miles, but not to become totally exhausted on a short, steep pitch because of insufficient traction. Nor is it acceptable to slow a group down continually while you are helped over hard parts, although it is proper and virtuous of the strong and well equipped not to walk off and leave the weak and inexperienced party member floundering on an icy patch like a bug sprayed with insecticide. All this fatigue can be avoided with good traction from a positive and secure traction device, which makes it possible to snowshoe on slopes as steep as the ones hiked in summer.

A beginner's tendency will probably be to shop for snowshoes and get the goodies such as traction later, to take a few hikes and see what works best and then get that item. This is sensible in a way, but overlooks one point: the less skill one has, the greater the need for extra traction. With experience one can foresee rough spots and place the snowshoes in such a way that they will hold; an expert in good physical condition can do

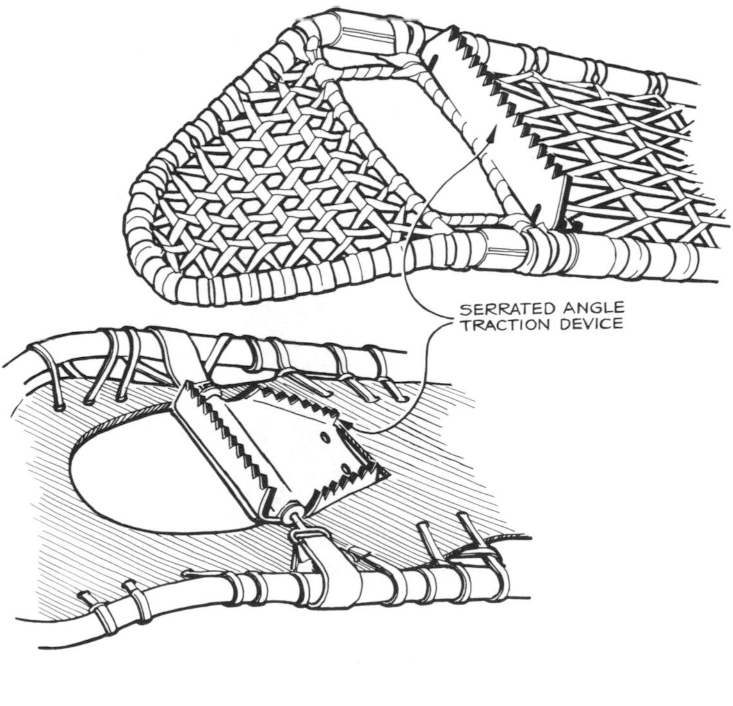

Fig. 17. Western snowshoes with serrated angle traction devices attached

amazing things with poor equipment. On the other hand, a beginner on the best of modern snowshoes and traction devices can make the old-timer with rope wrapped around his frames look very old indeed.

Another piece of equipment vital to maintaining balance in precarious positions is a ski pole or an ice axe with a ski-pole basket attached (Figure 18). The expert snowshoer can stand on one snowshoe on a steep slope and gracefully swing the other web around for a kick turn, but this may be impossible for a beginner. For both beginner and expert, the stability gained by using ski poles or ice axe with basket means easier traveling on difficult terrain and less fatigue to endure.

Heavy-duty poles, adjustable in length and with large baskets, are the type to buy. Downhill poles are better than nothing, but the small baskets sink much deeper than larger ones.

A good many snowshoers do not ski and do not have ski poles. Quite a number of mountain climbers snowshoe and so have ice axes, but this tool was of no use in deep, soft snow until someone bought a large basket for a GI ski pole and attached it to his ice axe, thus making it a practical part of a snowshoer's equipment. Ice axe baskets are now designed to be attached to

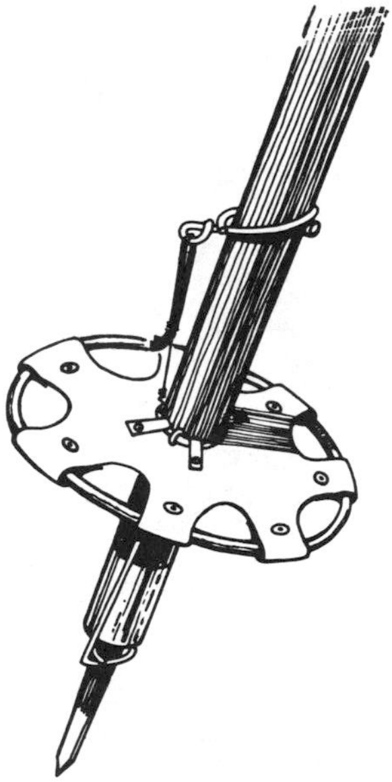

Fig. 18. Ice-axe basket

the ice axe without drilling holes, which weaken the shaft. One type uses a radiator hose-style clamp to tighten it to the shaft, requiring a screwdriver for installation or removal. Another has an elastic cord that hooks onto the glide ring stop and requires no tools at all. Be sure that the center hole in the basket is large enough to permit your axe shaft to slide through it—some are too small.

During very cold weather, the metal ice-axe head tends to chill the hand. A solution is to cement eighth-inch closed-cell foam on the head. Leaving the tip of the pick and adze uncovered makes the covering less likely to peel off when the axe is used to chop steps or level the tent platform.

The ice axe's use varies from region to region. Although generalizations are sometimes greatly in error, it appears that before water-ice climbing (climbing on ice formed from seeping springs) became popular, long ice axes were in vogue, especially in the West. These were used much as a cane on snow and glaciers, an extra leg when on unstable footing. By adding a ski pole basket to it, you could use this valuable extra leg in winter.

At present short axes are in style because they are the right length for water-ice climbing. It is fairly usual to see a short axe strapped to a pack while the person under the pack is having trouble with balance on a steep trail. A companion with a long ax equipped with a snow basket will have a much easier time, placing the point of the axe in strategic places to prevent slipping and maintain balance. Beginning snowshoers should consider buying a cheap long axe—one long enough to reach the ground with the elbow slightly bent—for snowshoeing and a short technical axe for ice climbing.

CHAPTER 4

Clothing

Mountains have great variation of slope and snow conditions, and just as the snowshoe best adapted to the widest range of conditions is the one to get, so must clothing be chosen. Mountain weather seems to change from one extreme to another. Each area of the snowbelt has a winter weather pattern considered "normal" by the natives. This pattern probably holds true 51 percent of the time, which leaves up to 49 percent that is not normal, which is my observation of normal winter weather.

I've mentioned getting rained on in New Hampshire, British Columbia, and Washington in one winter. This is not normal in two of these locations. So the solution seems to be this: Prepare for subzero weather but don't be surprised if a heat wave strikes, the temperature vaults to above freezing, and it rains. Keep things as simple as possible by using garments that are the most adaptable to extreme cold as well as water repellent.

In the East, "normal" winter temperatures are about 0°F with –5° to –10° at tree line and 20–30 mph wind on ridges and summits. The Canadian Rockies and interior British Columbia are about the same, but with less wind except on summits. The Rockies and associated ranges of the United States are similar, with warmer daytime temperatures toward the south. The Sierra probably won't have extreme cold as often as the ranges farther north. The wet, snowy Cascades generally are the warmest winter range mentioned.

Residents of western Wyoming, where the temperature has reached –60°F, feel they have the coldest minimum temper-

North of Mount Rainier in the Washington Cascade Range

ature. Minnesota, Wisconsin, and Michigan (especially the Upper Peninsula) have recorded minimums near –50°F—not as cold, but the locals feel the consistency of subfreezing temperatures in the region is noteworthy. Actually, conditions vary so much in winter that if you wait a few days or weeks, the type of weather you're looking for will probably come. Alaska and the Yukon require expeditions and are somewhat beyond the limits of snowshoeing described in this book.

Generalizations are hard to make, but as temperatures dip below 0°F, you are permitted fewer mistakes outdoors. Somewhere around –30°F in still air, any mistakes will probably result in frostbite or worse. With wind, similar damage occurs at higher temperatures because of the chill factor: in a stiff wind, the thermometer may read 10 or 15 above zero, but the effective temperature is –30°F.

Severity and duration of storms is probably more significant than minimum temperatures and maximum snowfall. Remember that the farther north you go, the shorter the winter days, generally the lower the temperature extreme, and the greater the length of storm. Snowshoers on day trips will be in valleys and on lower summits and will have much less concern about clothing and weather than if they were on longer treks or higher summits.

A system of clothing should be devised that is adaptable to extremes of temperature, yet light in weight and requiring only minutes to adjust. The exertion of climbing or breaking trail through deep, loose snow generates sweat. Moisture, from sweat or melting snow, is the greatest problem connected with keeping warm in winter.

Wool is no longer in complete possession of first choice for pants, mitts, socks, and cap. There are many dedicated wearers of wool clothing, so it will probably stay at the top of the list, but it now must share first place with synthetic garments.

Wool contains a springy fiber that retains trapped air and insulates well even when wet, making it a desirable fabric for outdoor clothing. Polypropylene provides comparable insulation, can be woven into any thickness, and has several advantages. It is not itchy or allergenic; is much more elastic, adding to the wearer's comfort; and wicks sweat away from your body better than wool.

The long-time choices in underwear are still available, and not everyone is into polypropylene and Lycra®. A wool-cotton mix doesn't cause the itching and irritation that wool does when next to some people's skin. A few of us enjoy the feel of all-wool long johns against the skin. Some prefer tops and bottoms made of a very thick weave of cotton. Fish net in cotton and wool tops and bottoms still has a place in winter clothing. For the high-budget person, silk and angora tops and bottoms can be found in the fancier shops and specialty mail-order catalogs.

Polypropylene garments originally designed for use as long-underwear tops and bottoms have been so comfortable to wear that they have led to a new system of dress, becoming shirts and pants for a number of snowshoers. Polypropylene is not windproof, just as wool is not, so these garments require that windproof outer clothing be worn over them for added warmth. Wind pants and parka may be quickly put on, or removed if you are getting too warm. Polypropylene undergarments also are more attractive than the Civil War vintage union suit with its drop or split seat, the ugliest garment ever conceived.

Some people wear jogging shorts over polypropylene bottoms for modesty and others sew the fly shut for the same reason. Some people wear them tight, some wear them loose. However they're worn, the polypropylene garments can serve as the foundation of a system of clothes that is quickly adjustable to temperature changes.

One drawback of this material is its ability to retain and intensify body odors. When switching from wool to polypropylene, you will also change from a wet-dog odor to the smell of ancient unwashed socks or a locker room. However, polypropylene is easier to wash and dry than wool.

Windproof and water-repellent outer garments have been improved and proven effective and durable in the last 10 years. Nylon-cotton material, the favorite for parkas in the 70s, is fast becoming second in popularity to nylon laminates such as Gore-Tex®. These laminates have a layer of plastic material with microscopic holes in it bonded to the nylon outer layer. Moisture vapor from your body may be vented through the holes and the fabric, while rain and melted snow, with larger droplets of water, will not pass through the holes in the plastic layer. It

Weathering winter atop Mount Adams in New Hampshire's Presidential Range

sounds impossible but actually works as well or better than any other water-repellent fabric. These must be kept clean to function properly.

A word of caution about buying waterproof, coated outer garments. Moisture from your body will condense inside the garment, usually as frost in winter, and get you as wet on a cold, dry day as if you were being rained on with a leaky jacket.

Some people need more insulation than polypropylene long underwear and a shell outer. The old standby of long underwear, heavy wool pants, and a shell outer may be their choice. Or they may wish to substitute insulated overpants for the shell windbreaker. Several types of thin, synthetic batting are quite effective in providing generous insulation without weight or bulk. Another option is wearing Lycra® tights under polypropylene bottoms, or wool pants, when a little more insulation is needed, but regular long johns are too much.

Whatever their material, the best outer pants should be easily adjustable in case you get too hot and are sweating. They should have full length zips so they can be put on or taken off with boots, crampons, or snowshoes on your feet. They can then be quickly removed when entering the tent or buildings, yet quickly put back on upon leaving the shelter.

Wool pants are still more popular than the polypropylene bottoms, in spite of what I consider their worst disadvantage. The heavier weight wool fabrics are usually rather shaggy, and snow sticks to them. Hard finish, high quality all-wool pants don't get covered with snow as badly but are difficult to find.

A real plus for nylon outers is that snow doesn't stick to them. You will stay drier on a bushwhack through snowy trees with nylon outers. The nylon may not catch on branches and get ripped as easily as wool does. All of us who have used (and still use) wool, can recall setting up camp in a snowstorm, then crawling into tent or snow shelter with pants coated with snow that couldn't be scraped off, and which likely melted onto the sleeping bag in the warmer shelter. This isn't the wisest planning!

When it comes to fit, some people prefer snug pants, although a loose fit has several advantages. Loose clothing makes it easier to step up higher, reach, stretch, and scramble and crawl through underbrush and thickets when bushwhacking. Choose clothing that won't inhibit your motion. Already the energy demand is much above that for traveling on bare ground.

Sometimes suspenders are more comfortable than a belt and work well to hold loose pants up; low-slung trousers with the crotch halfway down to your knees will make stepping up more difficult.

Tight clothes are also less warm than loose ones. Loose garments have an insulating layer of air between the clothes and your skin. Clothing tight against your body will be warmed, and any snow that gets on it will melt, dampening the garment and making the wet fabric a conductor to "suck" heat away from you.

Suspenders or knickers with long socks need some getting used to. After changing a sweater, first time users sometimes forget to put them back up on the shoulders until catching the dangling elastics on, say, a tree as they pass by. Knickers are stylish and have no bind over the knees as some long pants do, and are somewhat more effortless to walk in. However, the short pants have an air leak at the knee, which long pants do not have.

Down jackets or parkas have been the garment to put on when stopping for a break on the trail in cold weather, and the ultimate protection above tree line in subzero temperatures and wind. Down is first choice in cold dry climates, but if it gets wet, the down will mat and, like cotton, lose its insulating quality. Keep it in a waterproof stuff sack in your pack, and put a water-repellent shell over it if there is a chance of its getting wet.

In wet-winter areas, polyester batting, which has springy fibers like wool, is a better choice in a jacket or parka than down. It is available in various thicknesses. Several types of quilted insulating material with various trade names are available, varying in their prices and amount of warmth.

Polypropylene or wool mitts with shell outers are a versatile combination. Inners made of these fabrics combined with separate gauntlets are close to the equal of the down mitts traditionally regarded as the ultimate in warmth. The inners also can be dried more easily than down mitts.

Outer mitts, whether shell or insulated, should have waterproof, coated fabric on the palms and front of fingers and thumbs. Wear on this part of the mitt can quickly shred lighter weight fabric, laminate or nylon.

One of my favorite mitts is one piece but with a synthetic pile lining that can be pulled out for drying. It is available with a lightweight or heavyweight pile lining, the thick, fluffy weight for me being warmer than any down mitt because the pile doesn't compress as down does when I grip the ice ax. I always seem to be carrying an ax or climbing rope when the weather is coldest.

If there is a difference in durability, polypropylene has the edge over wool in socks and mitts. For both these garments, the elasticity of the polypropylene is of benefit. Lightweight mitts and gloves of polypropylene also are excellent for avoiding cold, bare hands and fingers when setting up the stove, or other jobs, allowing finger dexterity nearly precise enough to button buttons.

Never skimp on mitts and gloves. Your hands are vital in the winter outdoors, and everything you touch seems to be covered with snow.

It is important to have good headgear, since heat loss

from the uncovered head may be equal to the entire body heat production when at rest. The cap should be a combination face mask and stocking cap, large enough to pull down over the ears, or down to the neck when the weather is bad. Most face masks have eye holes, a nose hole, and a mouth hole. Better is one with a wide opening that can expose the face from eyebrows to chin, or be closed to cover mouth and nose, with goggles to protect the eyes.

Goggles are not practical on New England ridgetops when rime ice is freezing out of the clouds, because it ices over the goggles, too. In very windy subzero temperatures, care must be used when exhaling—moist breath can be whipped about by the wind to freeze on goggles and then must be scraped off. On a clear, brilliant day at high elevation on snow, sunglasses are necessary to prevent snow blindness. In high wind and below zero temperatures, a neoprene or leather face mask may be desirable. People with tender skin can get nipped on the cheeks or nose at 0°F and 10–15 mph wind. Covering the nose and mouth with the mask, so you breathe through a layer of wool, has advantages in severe cold and wind. It is a little sloppy when the wool gets soaked with moisture from the breath, but the exhaled air warms the wool, which in turn warms the next breath. The neoprene or leather face masks have small openings the breath goes through.

A homemade snorkel is useful in place of, or in addition to, the wool cap/face mask combination. This is a six- or eight-inch length of wool sock, with the toe cut off and open, used as a breathing tube. Place one end over the mouth and nose and leave the other end dangling. The sock should be large enough to reach from just below the eyes to well under the chin, with an elastic band over the head to hold it firmly in place. The snorkel is especially useful for sleeping. If the sleeping bag isn't quite warm enough, breathing cold air may be enough to cause you to spend a cold night.

It is important to discover how much clothing you need, as well as the temperature patterns of your area. By experimenting you can soon arrive at a combination that is adaptable to changing weather conditions without carrying too many pounds or spending too much money.

Gaiters are essential to cover the gap between pants cuff and boot top to keep snow out of the boots. There is less condensation under them if the upper part of the gaiter is of a breathable fabric, either a laminate or synthetic-cotton combination. The lower part should fit snug against your boot and be made of a heavy-duty, waterproof material. Coated is fine. Some styles fit pacs well and others are better for mountaineering boots. Make sure they fit before you buy.

Most gaiters have full-length zippers, perhaps covered by a flap that is held shut by snaps or Velcro®. Some have full-length Velcro® without the extra flap or zipper. The easiest to put on have the closure on the front where you can see it.

Some gaiters extend to the boot sole and have an elastic band sewn to the bottom, which holds it snug to the boot, and a band of the same elastic under the instep. These are warmer and more waterproof than the shorter gaiters.

Insulated or "super" gaiters are a must for cold temperatures and travel on snow, especially at subzero. They increase the warmth of a single climbing boot to near the equal of the double mountaineering boot. Most have a cable sewn into the hem at the bottom of the gaiter, which when tightened works into the groove between boot upper and sole, the "welt." Normally this is not as easy as putting on your regular gaiters, so the super gaiter is left on for several trips. A front zipper provides access to the boot laces.

Super gaiters never slip up over the boot when crampons or snowshoes are worn, since the straps of these items hold the gaiter on. However, kicking steps in snow without crampons is the stress that will push the gaiter up off the boot toe. The heel seldom slips up as the instep strap holds the gaiter on the boot heel quite well.

To prevent the gaiter from sliding up off the boot toe, cement a "lug" on the toe of the boot, just above the welt. Use jogging-shoe repair glue and a piece of plastic-coated household clothesline rope a quarter inch in diameter and two inches long. This will work well on plastic boots since they have a rough surface on the toe and heel to help hold super gaiters on the boot.

Super gaiters are essentially heavy-weight nylon-pack-cloth overboots that extend up to the knee. Some are insulated and feature lug soles; others have neither. The insulated types are meant to be worn over light summer boots and may provide a practical solution for people who want winter-quality footwear without having to buy double mountaineering boots.

Long gaiters are necessary with knickers, because the

long knicker socks, being of wool with a long nap, don't protect the lower leg from wind and become covered with snow, which melts. Knickers are comfortable, with little bind over the knee when you need to step very high, as is common in deep snow.

Keeping the feet warm isn't entirely up to the boots. If you have clothing on torso, legs, and arms adequate to keep all of them warm, probably mediocre cold-weather footgear will be sufficient. If your blood is warm as it flows through arms and legs, it will do a lot toward keeping feet and hands warm. But the warmest boots and mitts won't keep feet and hands warm if you are standing around in wet cotton pants and soaked shirt and jacket.

Two pairs of socks will provide both cushion and warmth. If wool irritates your skin, wear cotton or polypropylene next to your foot. For an overnight stay be sure to dry wet socks and carry extras. Wet clothing can be dried over a stove in a tent. Quite a bit of the warmth of leather boots is contributed by socks, so keep them as dry as possible. Lightweight leather boots are not adequate for cold weather, but if your boots are not warm enough don't try to solve the problem with more socks. It is possible to freeze your feet if the extra socks make the boots too tight and restrict the blood circulation. some people use skindivers' sealed-foam socks for cold weather, but since they are waterproof, they may cause discomfort by holding body moisture inside.

Of the several types of footgear used for snowshoeing, soft boots are probably the most popular for level terrain. The shoe pac with rubber lower and leather upper was designed in New England and has long been a favorite for snowshoes. With plenty of socks and insole or with a felt liner, these boots are warm enough for the severest subzero as well as above-freezing temperatures. Shoe pacs and snowmobile boots that are constructed of rubber lowers and leather or fabric uppers don't really provide sufficient support for the foot. When the bindings are tightened for mountain travel, the pressure is on the foot, rather than on the boot. Some people wouldn't use anything but shoe pacs, but for a person with really cold feet—like me—it takes a lot of socks, or a felt inner boot, to make them warm enough, and the binding will frequently bruise or blister the spots of greatest pressure (for blister treatment, see chapter 11).

Leather mountaineering boots are also quite popular for snowshoeing, and some insulated leather climbing boots are warm enough for winter use by people who don't have a cold-feet problem.

The warmest boot currently most available is probably the plastic double boot. Designed for mountaineering, the boot has a heavy lug sole and hard toe, so snowshoe or crampon bindings hold well and do not bruise the foot even when cinched down. These double boots are quite lightweight compared to the now nearly extinct leather model. The insulation is in the inner boot, similar to the felt liner in the pacs mentioned earlier. These inexpensive liners fit quite well in the plastic outer, and are probably warmer than the regular inner boot. The inner boots and socks will need to be dried each night as must be done with pacs, since the plastic outer boot is impervious as is the rubber or plastic bottom section of pacs.

Generally plastic double boots are comfortable, with a few exceptions. Be sure, if you intend to walk long distances in them, that the ankle is "hinged," permitting bending or flexing of the ankle.

Some people have suffered bruised and abraded shins. Be sure to lace the section up to the ankle very tight, and tie it. Treat the section above the ankle separately, leaving it as loose as possible. If bruising is still a problem, slit open the top of the tongue and pull out enough of the insulation to decrease the pressure on your shin.

The ultimate in cold-weather foot protection is the GI Korea boot, also called the Mickey Mouse, mouse, or bunny boot. It is still available at some military surplus stores but is becoming scarce in small sizes. The boot is made with rubber or synthetic outer and inner layers with about three-eighths of an inch of insulation sealed between. As long as the insulation stays dry the boot is incredibly warm and rates first for protecting climbers' feet from frostbite on such peaks as Alaska's Mt. McKinley. Most commercial insulated rubber boots are very soft and really not very warm. The chief complaint about the mouse boot is the waterproof inner layer, which prevents evaporation of sweat so completely that your socks will probably be soaked by the end of the day. After a couple of days of this type of immersion the skin is wrinkled, soft, easily blistered, and known locally as dishpan feet. You may prefer to change socks at midday.

Some mouse boots have a smooth liner of nylon and slide onto your foot easily. Those with an all-rubber interior are a different story. In the chill of a below-zero morning it's easy to lose your temper when the reeking boot adheres to your socks and you must pull so hard to get it on that you fear a hernia, ruptured spinal disc, and leg cramps—all at the same time. Tent interiors are cramped, so campers must take turns dressing. If your companion is fighting to get boots on, lie back and leave lots of room.

Heavy mountaineering boots and commercial insulated boots of leather are probably about equal in warmth. In temperatures of around 15°F they are borderline. When you are just standing around, your feet will likely begin to get cold. Snowshoe bindings must be adjusted fairly tight for good control, which restricts blood circulation in the feet and causes them to chill more quickly.

Be sure when camping out to use boots as a pillow or put them between sleeping bags or someplace else where they aren't chilled all night. Warming them in the sleeping bag before arising is unpleasant but often desirable. It's hard to get your feet warm after putting on boots with frost inside them from a frigid night.

Keep in mind that easy hikes on warm, sunny days require less of your clothing. If you don't get too far from the road, allow plenty of time and energy to get back to your car, keep an eye on the weather, and don't go out when it is below zero in cold country or 25°F in warmer areas, your risk isn't terribly great.

However, on high peaks and in remote country you are committed to several days. You've got to have equipment for the storm that might catch you out there. By way of comparison, a lot of people who drown never expected to get in the water; some unexpected event placed them there. Those who survive such sudden events were prepared for them.

Incidentally, improvisation is fine but it can be carried to extremes. Avoid equipment or gimmicks cobbled on to something you already have that doesn't work right. These inventions give the appearance of increasing the adaptability of gear to many situations but often are too complicated to be practical or require constant adjusting. Try to pick out clothing that you adjust only when it becomes extremely cold, extremely windy, or extremely warm. Time spent fussing with gear would be better saved for enjoying the scenery.

CHAPTER 5

Other Equipment

There are so many new models of tents, packs, sleeping bags, and stoves that it is difficult to keep up. The improvements have come so fast that many of us have outdated equipment only 10 years old. Rather than list everything available, this text will cover some basic things to look for. Consult equipment guides for detailed comparisons. Each writer has his favorites, which may not match your own.

Tents

For general use in winter where high winds are no problem there are so many tent designs that a choice appears difficult. However, it is of greatest importance to get the simplest pole assembly and the most room for the least weight. Snow travel is strenuous and you will be carrying enough gear without adding unnecessary ounces to the load.

The 1980s have seen a reversal of the trend toward large, heavy-duty and elaborate backpacking tents. Costs escalating above $500 for the top of the line apparently didn't generate mass sales. At this date the expensive, fancy models have become scarce. There are lots of two person, lightweight and inexpensive two or three season tents on the market. But you should not expect a tent under $100 to bear any snow load or wind!

High winds, found above tree line, and particularly in New England and the Adirondacks, will flatten tents that aren't expedition quality, and some that are adequate for Alaska and the Himalaya. Heavy snowfall will have the same effect, unless you get out and shovel the snow off before damage is done.

Use the skills of the pioneers in winter camping to choose a spot in which to camp. Set your tent up where the natural features such as forest or rock outcrop will provide wind protection. This is a calculated risk above tree line since winds are notorious for not blowing the way you would expect them to. To be honest, there is very little in the way of wind protection above tree line; it seems to blow everywhere, first one direction and later another, until all points of the compass have been used.

The majority of winter campers can pick forested places to camp that are protected from wind. Decisions such as this will ease the strain on your equipment budget.

If you do choose to buy an expedition-quality tent, keep in mind that not all expedition labels indicate better quality, however, so compare before buying. Real such tents will have much reinforcing on seams and corners and may be of heavier fabric, and so will weigh and cost more. The heavier fabric also may be more windproof and water repellent. Still, the lightweight tent can be protected by shoveling or shaking the load off during a heavy snowfall, and if you know the area and use the terrain to advantage, you won't need to lug a Himalayan-quality tent. Do remember, however, that sheltered places accumulate more snowfall than wind-blasted ridges and plateaus, so be prepared to dig out more often.

Most tents lose a great deal of space in a simple A-frame or pyramidal design because the walls sag inward unless the guy ropes are adjusted frequently. For example, a tent with a floor five feet wide and seven feet long is hardly adequate for two people when the tent walls sag. However, one-foot-high sidewalls add enough room so that the two can put all their gear in the tent overnight or bring in one more person without gear. A-frame walls that slope from ground level to ridgetop usually have guy ropes to help hold them out, but by morning they always seem to have stretched so that the frost-covered inside rubs on you when you get in and out of your sleeping bag.

The large pyramidal type suffers equally. The center pole is probably the greatest nuisance, although it is handy to tie a flashlight to for illumination since before-sunrise breakfast and after-dark dinner is the usual order of things in winter. A low-silhouette, modified pyramid design with about one-foot sidewalls is available. The weight per person is small and usable room is much more generous than the tall, sagging, traditional designs, although these are still popular and have been improved. Many people prefer a high tent in winter because it allows them to dress and cook more comfortably, especially on a trip of several days.

External frames, which are about the only new modification in tent design in the last 20 years, add more usable internal space. The advantage of more room offsets the debit of extra weight in poles. The frame makes it possible to hold the roof out so the lower third is like have an 18-inch vertical sidewall. This also eliminates the center pole and several outside guy ropes. All the sections of external frames are joined by slipping the small end of one into the large end of the next. Vital sections may get lost as the tent is collapsed and rolled up in the morning. The solution to this problem is to run a length of elastic shock cord through the hollow centers of each section, then attach it on the inside of each end section so that no piece can be misplaced (some models are made this way). If there is some tension on the shock cord it is easy to join the sections, especially when setting the tent up in a storm or after dark. If the tent has solid fiberglass pole sections, about all you can do is count carefully each time you take the tent down to be sure you have them all.

Quonset- and dome-design tents have become more popular recently. They have a low profile, which makes some models extremely wind resistant, and are surprisingly roomy inside for their small dimensions. Some very large and roomy geodesic-style tents are available that seem ideal for winter camping in sheltered areas since the weight per person is less than when using two-person tents.

The average modern tent is made of nylon rather than cotton. Nylon can be lightweight and nearly windproof, quite water repellent, and very strong. Coated fabrics have their problems: some are supposed to breathe but don't, and most coatings peel.

Laminated fabrics have received wide acceptance. Sealing the seams and keeping the fabric clean seem to be the key to its qualities of being waterproof against rain yet permeable to vapor from body and breath, which keeps the inside of the tent amazingly dry. By avoiding the need for a rain fly, which is almost a necessity for other tents in winter, you save a couple of pounds of weight.

My present winter tent is a quonset design made of laminated fabric. It does not leak in an all-night rainstorm and with some ventilation, moisture and frost do not condense inside down to 0°F. Below zero, frost appears overnight. Under some conditions, ice can cover the outside and stop the tent from breathing. The weight of 4½ pounds is good but headroom is poor. Putting on clothes in the morning is unpleasant with the frosty ceiling. However, no lightweight tent is going to be very roomy: for each plus factor of your equipment there is a compromise.

A rain fly is useful in near-melting or rainy winter weather, unless the tent is highly water repellent. Essentially a tarp shaped to tie over the tent, this second layer of fabric sheds moisture and adds warmth. It also can be used as an extra ground cover inside the tent or to cover gear left outside. (It is desirable to stow all packs inside the tent to keep them from being buried in snow, although a small tarp can be used to cover these items outside.)

Care must be used to protect your tent's waterproof floor from cuts and scrapes that let moisture in. Foam pads provide floor insulation and are a must instead of air mattresses and other unsuitable choices—such as boughs, which were vastly overrated even when considered environmentally acceptable. An improvement is the self-inflating air mattress, which is good down to –5° or –10°F. It is insulated as well as air-filled for comfort and requires only a few puffs to fill (the old noninsulated air mattress was actually a way to sleep colder). In subzero cold a foam pad above or below your air mattress will probably be a necessary addition.

Ventilation is required inside a tent, especially when you are cooking. Burning gasoline, kerosene, or propane releases not only poisonous fumes but a large amount of water vapor, which may condense on the tent ceiling. Boiling water adds to this. It is frustrating to be wet in a good tent that doesn't leak from the outside simply because cooking vapors and the occupants' moist breath create enough moisture to condense on the walls and drop on sleeping bags, occupants, *et al.*

Sleeping Bags

Choice of a sleeping bag for winter depends mainly on how much warmth you need. This probably will have to be guessed by experience on previous summer camping trips. For some people a bag with two pounds of down or polyester batting is sufficient, but others require double that plus an insulated jacket as a blanket.

The insulating value of the down or polyester is dependent on the amount of trapped air. Down is extremely lightweight, and when contained as in a sleeping bag, it has great insulating ability per pound of weight. Improved polyester-filled sleeping bags deserve consideration. Their weight is greater than down bags for equal warmth, but they cost less. The main advantage of this synthetic fiber over down is its ability to insulate when wet.

If there is no chance to dry your gear, moisture will build up in the sleeping bag when you are camping on snow for several nights. A down bag will quickly mat and lose warmth, unlike the synthetic fiber. A sleeping-bag cover of water-repellent laminate will help prevent moisture from condensing in the bag. Theoretically the moisture from your body will pass through the laminate and condense or freeze on the outside of the cover—but don't count on that happening consistently.

Sleeping bag manufacturers have written at great length on the relative warmth of different types of construction. All agree that when the two layers of cloth that contain the down or synthetic fiber are sewn-through or quilted, the insulating value is reduced. Next best is the system of inner and outer fabric separated by walls that in effect create separate tubes or boxes. These allow the down or synthetic to fluff, or loft, with no sewn-through part where the filling is compressed. The warmest bags are those in which the individual separating walls of the tubes overlap. This construction prevents all but a few cold spots.

Simplicity, warmth, and roominess are of greatest importance in the sleeping bag. Frequently you are chilled when first getting in the bag and so have removed only jacket and wind parka. Insulated bodies are crowded on each side and after a couple of hours you awaken, uncomfortably warm. If the bag is roomy enough, either pants or shirt, or both, may be removed without unzipping the bag. These garments may be put on again inside the bag without the discomfort of exposing a lightly clad body to the cold air next morning.

The penalty for warmth and comfort is usually weight and expense. It is pleasant to emerge fully dressed and warm from the insulated cocoon, hands warm and efficient for starting the stove. The Spartan can survive in a tight, lightweight bag, especially for only one night, but winter nights are about twice as long as summer nights. It is not unusual to crawl into bed at 8:00 P.M. or earlier and remain there until it is light outside at 7:00 A.M. or later. If you are uncomfortable, these are long, dismal hours to suffer through.

Getting into the sleeping bag with wet or moist clothing is a mixed blessing. You will eventually become warmer and your clothes will get dryer, but the sleeping bag will get wetter. Thus the warmth of the final backup system—the sleeping bag—is sacrificed. It's better in the long run to carry extra clothing in waterproof bags and change to dry garments before crawling into the bag. It is also better to strip and get in the bag naked rather than unnecessarily get your sleeping bag wet. You'll warm up faster that way, too, since you won't be using body heat to dry out your clothes. The initial shock of cold fabric on bare torso is severe but fortunately brief.

The greatest problem in keeping the sleeping bag dry in winter, of course, is using it in subfreezing temperatures. Your body puts out moisture as vapor, even while sleeping. The vapor condenses in the sleeping bag and is more evident when the weather is cloudy and close to raining or snowing. At times of falling rain or snow, the problem is unspeakable. If the winter trip involves packing up camp and moving each day with no chance for drying, the bag soon becomes noticeably moist and less warm. For this reason people in areas that are consistently humid in winter are replacing old down bags—as well as parkas—with polyester.

The most convenient way to dry the bag in winter is to have a bright, warm day that will heat the interior of the tent to the fifties or sixties. Wet gear laid out on pads will dry remarkably well in this manner. If it is possible to dry the sleeping bag and clothing on a sunny day or with a fire, do so. If moisture is of major concern on your winter outing, look into some polyester batting and pile garments. With the vast array of equipment available, there's no reason to sleep cold or carry too heavy a load. And have a back-up plan so if the weather is unusually wet and everyone's gear is getting moist, it is possible to end the outing early.

Some planning is necessary to counteract the moisture buildup in clothes and sleeping bags. Probably most people accept it on less than a week's trip, but three things will do a lot toward keeping you warm on a winter backpack.

First, your body rapidly adapts to cold and by the second

or third night will tolerate the cold with much less discomfort. Second, remove fewer clothes each night for sleeping if the chill is too great to ignore, and third, eat heavily before sleeping. A large helping of food high in sugar, eaten partway through the night, does wonders for keeping up body heat production. If you still can't sleep due to chill, remember that the old-timers used to do this with a wool blanket and a can of beans.

Winter campers in the colder places in the Snow Belt sometimes use a waterproof liner, called a vapor barrier, in their sleeping bags. This is used when temperature and wind chill are so far below zero that you know it's going to be colder than you are equipped for. The liner keeps the insulation in your sleeping bag dry because vapor from your body doesn't moisten it. Some hold that keeping the moisture in contact with your body also increases warmth.

A vapor barrier is probably an emergency measure because the amount of moisture that comes off your body in one night is both amazing and disgusting. Any clothing worn will be soaked by morning, so it's best to sleep nude. A towel is desirable as you emerge from the vapor barrier nearly as wet as after a shower and as smelly as an unwashed sock. You might want to try this at home first. The liner is a potential life-saver for people who enjoy winter camping in the really cold backcountry, and something that might be added to emergency equipment for any winter campers.

Most bags have a zipper opening with a hood. The hood is of course vital in cold weather and should have a simple drawstring to cinch it down when the zipper is entirely shut, leaving an opening only large enough to breathe through. It is a mistake to breathe inside the bag since breath is laden with moisture, which will cut the insulating value of the down or polyester. The snorkel—a six-inch length of wool sock held in place by elastic and used as a breathing tube—is a real help in sleeping; the exhaled air warms the wool, and the inhaled air is thus somewhat warmed. Breathing cold air severely chills the body.

Some otherwise excellent sleeping bags have added gimmicks that cut the warmth considerably. Long zippers tend to be cold, even when special tubes of insulation lap over them. Some are designed to be zipped onto another bag to create a double bag for two, but generally these combinations sacrifice warmth and add weight and cost. Others have special drawstrings on the hood, including one around the neck. The last thing I need in my sleeping bag is a tight cord around my neck. Sometimes in winter the tent or snow cave seems confining. Falling snow packs against tent walls, further constricting already tight quarters. Great piles of snow falling out of trees hit the surface with dull thuds that make sound sleep difficult. Wind flaps the tent, adding another irritation. Snowshoers have been known to have nightmares under such circumstances and rip their way out of the sleeping bag with appropriate grunts and snarls. The noose around the neck might be a handicap at such a time.

Packs

You will need something big enough to carry the clothing and extras necessary for a winter outing. A pack with a huge sack is better than a small rucksack jammed so full it is hard to find things. It takes more equipment to hike in the winter than in summer, whether on a one-day hike or overnight. If it is all inside the bag, it won't get as snowy as it will tied on the outside of an undersized pack.

There are many styles of packs with a wide range of prices. The more expensive ones are usually lighter in weight and made of waterproof nylon fabric. The most valuable qualities are durability (so the pack will not fall apart and require time for repairs), plenty of room inside the main bag (so there will be no need to tie things on the outside), padded shoulder and hip straps (to support weight comfortably), several outside pockets (for goggles, compass, snacks, canteen, moleskin, and other frequently used items), waterproof fabric (so the gear inside will not get wet in a storm), and a large top flap (to completely cover the top opening and keep rain and snow from working in).

There are three basic kinds of packs: those with an external frame, those with an internal frame, and those without a frame (soft packs).

The purpose of the frame, often made of lightweight aluminum or fiberglass, is to provide a rigid platform for attaching straps and bag. Wide straps hold the frame away from the wearer's body. Shoulder straps attach just above the center of the external or internal frame and again at the lower corners. The hip strap is also attached at both sides of the lower points of the frame.

The newest addition is the extremely large—5000+-cubic-inch capacity—internal-frame packs. More development work has been done on these than the old, standard external-frame packs. The largest of these new internal-frame models will hold enough gear for a week's camping in winter. The cost is in direct proportion to the size.

The internal frame is simpler and less bulky than the external frame, so the internal frame pack rides closer to the wearer's body. Some external frames extend above your head, others are wider than your body, and some wrap halfway around your hips.

The soft pack depends for its rigidity on the way its load is packed. Sleeping bag, clothing, and soft items obviously will claim the side next to the wearer's back to protect shoulder blades and spine from such sharp objects as stove and food containers. The pack rides against your body from hips to neck, or above, depending on how much gear you take. Padded shoulder straps and hip strap complete the soft touch against your body. They have more give and don't abrade the arms as the frame pack does when taking it off or putting it on.

Choose a pack that will do the most things the best for you. Avoid the medicine show-type pack with sleeping bag, pots and pans, and camp shoes strapped on the outside and extending above your head when snowshoeing in rugged terrain. Winter backpacking trips often are to a location where camp is set up and day trips are taken from there. Some people put a small daybag in the pack to use for the shorter trips, although it may weigh three pounds or more—nearly as much as the sleeping bag. If possible, find a large backpack that is comfortable and also usable for the day hikes to save carrying the extra pounds.

Proper fit of packs makes breathing easier: a heavy load on the shoulders impedes breathing and cuts down on the air supply to the lungs, which in turn slows down the flow of nourishment to the blood and increases fatigue. Frame packs can be adjusted to fit almost any size person comfortably. The shoulder straps should be shortened or lengthened to carry the load without being so tight that the frame bruises the back or so loose that the back strap hangs down on the buttocks. The wide web strap across the lower part of the frame should rest on or just below the belt or waistband of the pants, usually a little below rather than above.

When this is accomplished, hunch the shoulders slightly

Delving into the pack for a quick snack in Washington's eastern Cascades

to raise the pack and tighten the hip strap attached to the bottom of the frame. This strap should buckle below the pants belt and above the crotch on the lower abdomen, about where low-slung pants ride. All is in proper adjustment when the weight of the pack is carried partly on the shoulder straps and partly on the hip strap, thereby taking the strain off the shoulder muscles. Adjust a soft pack the same way.

Whatever pack you choose, learn to pack it and adjust it and carry it efficiently on whatever terrain you are on. In other words, make sure that you know how far it sticks up, out, and behind so you don't get stuck in narrow places and that you can sit down and scoot yourself down a steep place without the pack's forcing you over frontwards. (Many trees fall in winter in thick forest and must be climbed over or squeezed under.)

It's also annoying to the rest of the party if one person

must constantly stop to adjust shoulder straps, rearrange a hard object, or delve deep into the main compartment to locate a snack. Especially when he has the Twentieth Century Special with nine outside pockets, five zippered compartments, and an extension sleeve on the top that doubles as a bivouac bag in case of storm. The middle of a snowshoe trail is not the place to out-fumble your companions.

Stoves

The stove has gained importance because wood fires have become impractical—and often illegal—for hikers and climbers to use. This is probably more a benefit than a drawback since winter forests don't necessarily have large quantities of easily obtained dry wood. In fact, as more people use the mountains and backcountry for year-round recreation, the supply of firewood in popular places has, for all practical purposes, been used up.

In winter the stove is used a great deal more than in summer. Usually snow must be melted for water because streams are either too deeply buried under snow or frozen over. The stove's quality, therefore, takes on a great deal of importance.

The first two requirements are that the stove put out lots of heat and that it have a large base so that when a two-quart container of snow is melted to water it won't easily be tipped over on the sleeping bags.

The fuel container should be simple to refill since fuel requirements in winter are higher than those in summer. For my style of cooking, a quart of white gas is adequate for two people for a week's outing, melting all water from snow; I carry a pint extra in case we use more. Some people will need twice as much fuel as I use, so be careful not to leave yourself short.

The stove should have a pump so it can be pressurized quickly. Stoves without pumps must be warmed by hand or primed to develop pressure, and warming your cold stove by hand in winter can be unpleasant and even result in frostbite.

Three U.S.-made stoves have been used extensively the past 10 to 15 years and are quite dependable. All three put out lots of heat, are fairly fuel efficient, light easily, and have good pumps.

Two of the stoves use standard pint or quart (half or one

liter) fuel bottles that are connected to the burner section by flexible or rigid tubing and a fitting that screws into the bottle. Because their heat-regulation valves are not delicate, usually allowing only settings of high-heat or off, these two include a metal disc you can place on the burner to reduce the heat. Both stoves are lightweight and can be dismantled for carrying in the pack; care must be used to keep dirt out of the system.

The third stove has a large fuel tank with a burner attached to its top. Its fuel valve permits regulation of the heat. Because it has solid legs, it provides more stability when holding large pots. The trade-off for this solid construction is bulkiness.

The larger foreign-made stoves are also popular in winter. Often seen are those that fold into a sturdy metal container. These can be obtained with pint or larger fuel capacity. They are the fastest to set up to cook with, and to fold up to place in the pack. When the container hinges open, the fuel tank is in one side of the case and the burner separated and ready to be lit in the other side. These are well protected inside the container when folded up.

The drawbacks of most stoves are either heavy weight or the need to refill the tank frequently. However, if the cook is careful to top off the tank after the evening meal, it is all set to go for breakfast. A large tank should last several days, and experience will indicate when the tank needs refilling.

The key to cooking on any stove is planning and getting expert at starting, refilling, repairing, and adjusting the pressure and flame on your stove. There are many older-design stoves that are still working perfectly well. Some people use the 1920-style stoves that have no adjusting valve, but by pumping in more pressure or bleeding off pressure the flame is set at high for melting snow or low for simmering the bacon. These stoves must be dismantled, with the potholders removed, the burner screwed off with the wrench that is included, a metal stopper screwed in to close that hole, and the parts then packed in a metal case for carrying.

There are many stoves without pumps used for winter, and even in subzero temperatures. Again, planning is the key. The whole stove is warmed inside the parka or sleeping bag before opening the valve. The warming increases the pressure in the tank so the fuel is forced out to the burner when the valve is cracked open.

White gas is probably the best fuel. Kerosene is harder to prime to start, but otherwise is about equal to white gas. Sometimes the burner must be primed twice before it is hot enough to ignite and burn cleanly. Propane and butane gas are poor choices in winter. Cold temperatures prevent the compressed gas from vaporizing and heat output is usually very poor—a large candle will often yield as much heat when the temperature is below zero. Extra gas and kerosene are both more compact and weigh less than the equivalent compressed gas cartridges, which of course must be packed out.

Some people make propane or butane cartridge stoves work in subzero cold. The favorite method is to place the whole stove in a cooking pot, which reflects heat back to the cartridge. Sometimes two stoves are put in the pot, with a large snow container on top of both. The combined heat reflection usually brings the temperature of the fuel high enough to vaporize and work very well.

Practice starting your stove before going on a trip to make sure it works properly and that you know how to operate it. Gasoline stoves are especially dangerous. All must be preheated so the burners vaporize the fuel before it squirts under pressure from the orifice. This is why you must burn enough fuel in the priming cup below the burner to adequately preheat the burner. If the valve is opened too soon, the gasoline is not vaporized and flaming liquid gasoline squirts out. Quick action is needed to close the valve as it is easy to run the priming cup over, resulting in a small amount of flaming gas on the floor of the tent—and a possible flash tent fire that could turn a mountain outing into a disaster. The tent is the one abode that is susceptible to man's oldest enemy—uncontrolled fire. Practice lighting the stove before the trip so you know what you are doing when igniting it in cramped and flammable quarters. Always leave the tent door open during the operation. Ventilation is desirable, and if the stove starts spewing flaming gasoline and you can't shut it off, throw it out in the snow.

Propane stoves are less likely to flare up because the fuel is already vaporized before it gets to the burner, so it ignites immediately. However, it is possible to fill the tent full of fumes if the valve is opened before the matches are ready, which could create an explosion and fire.

Kerosene is less dangerous but no less damaging if spilled fuel is ignited. Unlike gasoline, liquid kerosene doesn't burn with a hot enough flame to preheat its own burner. If the burner has not been heated enough, the flame is sickly yellow with lots of smoke. When preheated adequately, kerosene burns with a clean blue flame. Lighter fluid makes the safest priming fluid; it is much less volatile than white gas and comes in spill-proof cans with accurate pouring spouts. Alcohol is also good.

Use a piece of fireproof foam material as a stove base so the stove does not come into contact with the tent floor and possibly melt it. No matter what type of stove you use, be wide awake and alert before lighting it and always carry a "pricker" to clean the burner orifice if it carbons up and plugs. Make sure your fuel is clean. Have plenty of matches in case your easy-starting "pet" stove becomes reluctant with no warning, and there is no back-up stove in the group. Be very careful to keep dirt out of stoves that must be dismantled for carrying. Check pump leathers and gaskets frequently; they need to be replaced periodically. Stove failures in winter are likely to be a result of operator error or carelessness.

A large, stable stove that has a burner large enough to melt quantities of snow rapidly has advantages, but it will be heavy. This category includes most of the kerosene-burning models and some gas ones, which fold quickly into protective metal cases. Most kerosene models must be dismantled for carrying but weigh less than the folding stoves, which often have a very heavy case.

Some small, very lightweight stoves have quite large burners and will put out a great deal of heat for their size. Although a nuisance, you can save weight by planning to refill the small stove often rather than use the large one with a large-capacity fuel tank. A large stove probably melts as much snow as two small ones and weighs about the same (which presumably comes out even in cooking efficiency), but it will support a container three times larger than a small stove will, with less danger of spillage. There are proponents of both large/heavy/stable and small/light/unstable stoves loose in the hills, and no attempt will be made here to arbitrate. The intricacies of actually cooking in the tent are discussed in chapter 12.

Ski poles and ice axe are necessary aids for maintaining balance on steep slopes or in soft, deep snow.

SECTION 2

Technique

CHAPTER 6

Physical Conditioning

Most people enjoy an activity until they become tired, and the more strenuous the activity, the sooner fatigue detracts from enjoyment. Actually, few people enjoy snowshoeing for itself. Almost everyone who snowshoes loves the winter outdoors, which offers aesthetic, emotional, or even sensual pleasures. They enjoy the beauty; the sense of being humble in the presence of magnificent mountains; the clean, crisp atmosphere of unspoiled wilderness; and the exultation of reaching a difficult objective. Snowshoes are merely the means of getting out into the natural scene rather than viewing it from a distance.

Physical fatigue not only spoils the fun of an outing but may create danger by clouding perception and judgment. Tired parties may choose an apparently less strenuous return route only to find that fatigue-influenced shortcuts or alternatives become extremely dangerous or impossible routes.

Realistically, good physical condition is the best safeguard against emergencies. By conditioning you recognize your limits. You are more likely to avoid fatigue-caused errors because your mind is clearer. You will know when it is time to turn back because you have tested yourself and know whether you can make it back. And if you can't, you can start building a shelter so that tomorrow, after some rest, you can start out early.

Even someone used to summer backpacking may overestimate winter abilities. Snowshoeing is tiring in a number of ways—first, because it is hard to get a snowshoe to bite into the snow as firmly as a lug sole grips the solid dirt or rock of a sum-

Snowshoeing on windswept slopes near the summit of Mount Whitney, in California's Sierra Nevada

mer trail. There is some slippage almost every step, even with the best of traction: it's step up two, slide back one. Breaking trail through fresh snow takes lots of effort as the snowshoe compresses it 6 to 10 inches each step. At times half a mile an hour on a gentle trail is a fast pace; other times three miles an hour may be possible for several hours.

A day in near-zero temperature has a numbing effect on people unaccustomed to being outdoors in winter, and gusty wind adds another energy drain. Cold plus wind equal wind chill to living flesh and a resultant call on the body to turn up the thermostat. We pay for the winter outing with greater fatigue than the same outing exacts in summer.

Not only is footing poor and weather fatiguing, there are two additional burdens the body carries when snowshoeing: the weight carried on the feet and that carried on the back. The British Everest formula suggests that the weight of snowshoes on the feet may be as tiring as carrying a 40-pound pack. And the extra clothing and gear necessary to be comfortable in winter often amounts to 25 pounds for a day hike; in summer this weight would be adequate for overnight.

Snowshoeing puts an extra strain on a tendon in front of the hip joint. This tendon lifts the leg, and due to the slightly spraddled stance required to compensate for the width of the snowshoes, it is under unusual strain. The wider the snowshoe, the greater the strain. Compounding the problem is the high leg-lift necessary to snowshoe through deep, soft snow (Figure 19).

Midwinter trail-breaking in rolling country in northern Minnesota and east to Lake Superior is a good example of this. Snow may be six to eight feet deep, and consistent cold keeps it fairly soft and powdery. Snowshoes 11 × 57 inches are a favorite and are necessary to keep from sinking in very deep. This is in contrast to mountain areas, where steep slopes and firmer snow permit much smaller snowshoes.

When traversing sidehills, the uphill leg must be lifted higher than the downhill one, as the uphill snowshoe cuts more deeply into the snow in breaking out a trail. In snow conditions in which you walk in two trails, one slightly lower than the other, the uphill leg tires faster since it cannot be straightened out and relaxed with each step, but remains bent most of the time (Figure 23).

Traversing is mainly a technique used in the West in soft

Fig. 19. Traversing steep, deep snow requires extremely high lift of uphill leg.

snow where snowshoe steps must be fairly far apart so the higher step won't be weakened by the one below and collapse. Unfortunately, taking long steps uphill is not the way to conserve energy. In the East the preferred technique for slopes is to kick steps (Figure 25) and go straight up, usually punching through a crust too weak to "bare-boot" (snowshoe jargon for take off the snowshoes and kick steps). Often in the East there is not much base under the snow until late winter. By contrast, Cascade snow firms up and steep south-facing slopes often can be bare-booted in warm spells all winter long. (If your snowshoe sinks through the snow clear to the ground, there is no base. When you don't sink to the ground but are on packed snow, there is a base at that depth.)

Deep powder on steep mountainsides in British Columbia creates different problems from deep Cascade snow, which is usually fairly moist and so packs into firm steps. The cold powder snow farther north will pack, but it takes 20 to 30 minutes and is called age hardening. The snowshoe party doesn't get much benefit from the trail-breaker in the Canadian wilds.

Even after several people have gone by, each person may be sinking a little deeper on especially steep places and slipping in unconsolidated snow. Steps kicked straight up in powder snow in cold temperatures are very fragile. Often the first person has less trouble than the ones following as steps break out, and the line of steps may become a trench a foot or more deep, straight uphill.

Easterners scramble on crust more than they kick steps in it, and they rarely make switchbacks. This fixation on going straight up is partly because of the type of forest cover. Generally the trees are so close together it's impossible to find a decent route on switchback. If you've got to scramble through trees, the shortest route minimizes misery. Western forests tend to become more open and timber line is a zone.

For example, timber line in the Cascades is 6000 to 7000 feet, depending on which side of the range you are on. The upper limit of trees is lower on north slopes as snow lies there longer in the spring, higher on the east side of the range. Often there is a zone of about 1000 feet, starting around 5500 feet, where the forest thins and dwindles to a few bushes or stunted trees. The same 1000-foot zone is found in the Rockies, but the timber line is much higher, extending to 12,000 feet and above in places.

Only in the eastern United States—in the Adirondacks and New England—does heavy timber continue to so definite a line at a precise elevation on the windward side of the peaks. This line appears to be the lower limit of the subzero winds that originate in the Canadian arctic.

The open upper slopes of the West are ideal terrain for switchbacking. But in the East there is no room to work out the route, so it's go straight up or go home.

Scrambling on crust is strenuous even with snowshoe crampons. A couple of inches of powder snow keeps the points from biting in to their full depth, so some of the ascents above cliffs can be quite tense.

Snowshoers also have to struggle through patches of brush like the classic New Hampshire bushwhack up Lafayette Brook to Mt. Lafayette, highest point on Franconia Ridge. The thickets usually alternate with open forest buried in deep powder snow so it's impractical to take off snowshoes to thrash through the brush, as they must be put right back on.

Pulling yourself through tree-line Krummholz on snowshoes means lots of arm and shoulder strain. The epic exhaustion situation is to fall into an eastern spruce trap. Powder snow drifts over shoulder-high tree-line conifers so their tops are covered, but it's really hollow under the interlacing branches of two or more trees. You go clear to the ground with one snowshoe on top of the other and 15 pounds of snow on top of that. There's nothing to grab but powder snow and flimsy treetops so it's a grunt and groan struggle equal to a rock climber's strenuous 5.8 rock pitch to clamber out. Local legend has it that a tribe of dwarfs live under these trees and wrap chains around the ankles of the hapless victims of spruce traps.

It is obvious that on snowshoes, the feet must point in the same direction as the snowshoes, especially if the bindings are good. This makes for strenuous, repetitive motion. By contrast, when hiking on a summer trail it is possible to rest the feet and ankles by changing the direction they point. When hiking cross-country some people go to great lengths to vary their foot position, climbing steep slopes pigeon-toed or splayfooted, or side-stepping, first right side, then left side toward the hill. Most of these techniques are impractical on snowshoes, and the lower legs and ankles reflect the strain.

One last ache deserves mention. Rising on the balls of the feet when going uphill tires the calf muscles. However, letting the heel sag down flat on the snowshoe webbing stretches this muscle. Either technique results in some leg fatigue.

Anyone who climbs or hikes each weekend won't find it as necessary to condition. Most people, however, do not have that much free time. And the weather in late October, November, and early December is often wet and cloudy, which curtails hiking and climbing but doesn't provide enough snow for snowshoeing. It is this late autumn and early winter period of forced absence from the hills that makes it necessary for almost everyone to condition muscles, heart, and lungs so that preliminary outings can be made with a minimum of discomfort.

Probably the most effective dry-ground conditioning for snowshoeing is to wear the heaviest boots available while carrying a loaded pack—25 to 50 pounds for an adult. The leg muscles must carry the added weight of the heavy footgear in addition to the load on the back. Bending over to balance the load and straining each step comes close to duplicating the stance of the snowshoer struggling through deep snow. There is no need to carry a heavy load each time; you will still get good conditioning for a winter overnight hike or climb.

In most areas, there is some sort of rise for conditioning available within a short drive. As a last resort there are stairs, preferably outside. Many areas have favorite local hills used for conditioning hikes, some with organized speed events. But while this speed training is great for heart, lungs, and legs, it is not really similar to an 8- to 10-hour snowshoe trip. Speed in itself carries over poorly from dry trail to snowshoeing, largely because in aiming for greater speed, sprinters carry less load; T-shirt, shorts, and running shoes are their usual garb.

On the other hand, a heavy load forces the slow pace and swaying movement typical of snowshoe travelers. Heavy boots or ankle weights are about as close as you can come to duplicating the effect of snowshoes. Climbing hills with a heavy load in the pack and on the feet conditions the body to the type of strain that snowshoeing puts on it. The lungs must absorb oxygen into the blood stream and the heart pumps this energy-producing material to replenish the muscles, while the shoulders are burdened down and the rib cage constricted by the load.

Good conditioning for snowshoeing is a relative thing. The dedicated mountaineer and backpacker no doubt tries for a much higher level than the office worker who has no extensive background of trail-hiking experience. Some people will never desire more than a level snowshoe hike of a few miles. Thus a conditioning program will vary to suit individual ambitions.

Any type of conditioning—jogging, calisthenics, or whatever—is tiring for the weak and boring for the strong. But suffering through a conditioning program will make the mountain hikes fun—be miserable on the conditioning hill so you can enjoy the entire winter. After you have worked hard and forced your body to be strong, it will respond to your desires on a snowshoe outing, even when the going is difficult. Following is a fitness program for snowshoers who would like to climb major peaks in winter; it can be scaled down proportionately for lesser objectives.

Twice a week, take a conditioning hike (in the evening if necessary). Allow 50 to 75 minutes for a 1500-foot elevation gain on bare ground. When conditioning on snow on a packed trail, allow more time to compensate for poor footing. If you are conditioning on snow on snowshoes, you have probably achieved the discipline necessary to do strenuous snowshoeing! Use heavy boots and, depending on your body weight, up to 50 pounds in the pack (use rocks or containers of water). Descend without load since knees don't need this much stress on a practice hill. Repeat until this can be accomplished without special rest afterward. Every second or third trip take no load as a "bonus." After two or three weeks, cut down to one hike a week. Add a short mountain hike or climb every other weekend, building toward more strenuous hikes in six weeks or two months.

Variety is important. Do some rock climbing, especially if there's a desert nearby to provide a change from an all-snow recreation diet. New England and Rocky Mountain climbers have frozen waterfalls and iced-up slabs nearby. Practice some ice climbing. This is good practice in the East since a number of peaks have fun approaches involving bushwhacking and cramponing up slides. Snowshoeing is so dominantly a leg activity that there is a tendency to let the arms and shoulders just go along for the ride. Use these other activities to keep your upper body in tone, too.

It will become obvious that certain muscles are stressed by snowshoeing. A program of 10 minutes a day of calisthenics to strengthen these areas can help you get set for strenuous outings, even though you've never done it before. Calisthenics are especially helpful if you're tied to a desk job. It's a good way to begin the day if done upon rising in an unheated bedroom. Begin gently and work up to the following:

—50 sit-ups. Stretch to touch the toes.

—10 push-ups.

—10 leg-lifts each side. Lift the leg as high as possible, then extend the foot straight out.

—20 ankle flexes, Rise up on balls of feet as high as possible with a one-inch-thick book under balls of feet and heels on floor.

A recent development is the availability of exercise equipment in public facilities and clubs in small towns as well as in large cities. The training machines have a much lower quotient of boredom than calisthenics, so they will provide better conditioning for the time spent. The stair-climbing devices have a very high transfer in replicating climbing hills and mountains. Bicycle riding—especially pumping standing up, which is almost exactly the motion of the stair machine—does the same. When fall and winter weather is too wet, cold, or otherwise unspeakably atrocious for hiking or biking, one can retreat to a gym setting and maintain good snowshoeing condition.

Adjust to what is possible for your age and condition. It doesn't take as long to do these in a cold room and does wonders for warming your chilled body and increasing your tolerance for cold weather. Maybe you'll even develop one of those gorgeous bodies we see in the movies.

Also do stretching, especially of the hamstrings—the muscles in the back of the thigh. Increased flexibility is of benefit when snowshoeing. The larger footgear demands that at times you will take longer steps and have the feet much farther apart.

The purpose of this program is to build good hiking and climbing condition and maintain it year-round. It is much less painful to recondition after a short layoff than after a 20-year period of inactivity. Don't try to do it all at once like an over-eager youngster. If you are 40 and haven't done anything very athletic since your teens, be patient. If it took you 20 years to attain the degree of physical weakness typical of age 40, it will take a while to reverse the process. If you suspect some heart trouble or any serious physical weakness, have a complete physical examination before starting the program. Each hunting season finds a few weekend warriors whose enthusiasm exceeds the strength of the flesh to the extent that they expire. So begin slowly. The carcass you reclaim may, with care, be able to carry you far enough back into the hills to give you a new vision of the loveliness of winter hills and the worthwhileness of making the effort to get out and see them. If you can get the vision of yourself walking through areas where all evidence of man has been erased by deep snow, enjoying the clean, crisp, sparkling air, there is hope. There is a life to live that is richer and fuller if you can get away from the urban scene.

CHAPTER 7

Walking on Snowshoes

Snowshoeing is basically walking: you just strap on your snowshoes and walk away. But there are two important differences. First, the surface is inconsistent—stable and solid, or hard and slippery, or soft and bottomless—and all movements must reflect the condition of the snow. When traction is poor or position precarious, move very gently, with the flowing, fluid movement of a cat stalking a mouse. Don't lunge or leap from step to step, especially on a steep climb or traverse or when making a kick turn, and don't thrust forward so hard that your snowshoe slips backward. Even on a crust, continue to move more gently than you would on dry ground. Deep traction devices are a great aid, but often there is an icy spot in the midst of acres of firm snow, and this may cause an unexpected slip. Even the deepest traction does not grip on four to five inches of powder snow on a crust, where the soft snow on top may be too deep for the traction to cut through to the crust below.

The second difference in walking on snow is that the snowshoes are longer, wider, heavier, and more unwieldly than hiking boots. It takes some time to condition leg muscles to the wider stance. When walking slowly you center your weight alternately over the right and then the left foot. To thus balance on one foot you must move your upper body first a couple of inches left, then a couple of inches right with each step. Snowshoes emphasize this action. The extra weight on the feet tends to cause the snowshoer to take a longer, slower stride than normal, part of the adjustment to walking on snowshoes without undue fatigue.

When snowshoeing uphill, you need a longer stride because in loose snow it is necessary to step far enough that the new step is not undermined by the previous one, especially if the steps sink eight inches or so into the snow. Short, choppy steps tend to cause a lunge and an unnecessary slip. The effect on a traverse is that the tail of the forward snowshoe slides into the previous step, and any slip results in some sliding downhill. Usually this is of no consequence, but if the route goes through a narrow slot between two trees, even a slight misstep can dump the unwary into the tree hole below.

Generally the ice axe is used as a walking stick on level going. On hillsides it should be in the hand on the uphill side: unless you have a long ice axe, the axe is usually too short to use on the downhill side for balance. Sometimes it is best to lean on the axe just a little on a sidehill to make sure you don't accidentally overbalance, but it is easy to quickly shift it to the downhill side if necessary to prevent slipping. Ski poles require a little more planning to use efficiently because they are longer than an axe and require more time to place accurately. For level going, never bring the baskets ahead of the feet; actually push on the poles like a cross-country skier, which will help propel you along. Carrying a generous portion of your weight on the poles eases the strain on the legs, and a good high leg lift, necessary for breaking trail in deep, soft snow, is easier to achieve.

The greatest energy-saver, and a vital aid to pacing yourself, is the rest step, a momentary pause between steps. With a little practice you can adjust the length of the pause to the state of your fatigue. As you step forward, thrust the front snowshoe out and let it plop down, or stamp it firmly into place. Straighten —lock—the rear knee joint so the tendons and cartilage are holding your weight; pause and relax the thigh muscles, using the poles or axe to maintain balance. Bringing the rear leg ahead, thrust the snowshoe out, place it, lock what is now the rear leg, relax momentarily, and repeat. The effect is to rest the legs during the time they are actually working hard. A couple of seconds of work, a couple of seconds of rest, makes it possible to keep going steadily without long stops during which extra clothing must be dug out of the pack to prevent chilling. The rest step is a real help when climbing and breaking trail in deep, loose snow, which requires a high leg lift, with special strain on the tendons in the hip area. The brief rest between steps does more good than infrequent long sitting-down rests.

The pause during the rest step works to advantage in loose snow for another reason. The snowshoe is moved forward and stamped down, then after a pause you move gently forward and put your weight on it as the other snowshoe is moved forward and stamped into the snow. By stamping the snowshoe down, you accomplish two things. First, the snow is packed somewhat: even powder snow will firm up—the beginning of age hardening—if there is a pause between placing the snowshoe and putting weight on it. If it is done in one motion without pause, you will sink deeper because it will pack at a greater depth as your full body weight comes down. Second, the snowshoe cuts into the snow and grips it, not only with the traction device, but also with the crosspieces and webbing. Try to pack the steps at turns and other crucial points.

Take turns breaking trail. In loose snow the trail-breaker may have several extra pounds of snow on his snowshoes. This isn't balled or stuck on; it just falls on top of the webs when he sinks perhaps 8 or 10 inches.

Sometimes it is possible to break trail for five minutes continuously when climbing steeply in loose, deep snow; other times it may have to be reduced to as little as two minutes before changing leaders. This system makes it possible for each person to really force the pace for a few minutes while he is breaking trail. If there are five people taking turns, each will get 12 minutes rest between three-minute turns in the lead. As the time for breaking trail ends, the leader steps out of the way and drops to the rear as the rest of the party moves on past.

Most western mountain areas where snowshoeing is popular are different from eastern mountains in snowfall pattern and forest cover. Generally snowfall is heavier, so snowshoers have soft snow to travel on. Second, the westerners ascend ridges in switchbacks carefully engineered to create an inclined plane up which the hikers move steadily and consistently (Figure 20). This is in contrast to that classic section of the Appalachian Trail through Mahoosuc Notch and on up Mahoosuc Arm, which apparently seeks out the hard way.

The more open western forests lend themselves to a switchbacking snowshoe trail. Frequently deep snow hides the real trail, so snowshoers pick their own routes from open space to open space—which doesn't seem to exist in the East. Steep mountain slopes above timber line in the West are frequently wind-packed or firmed up by the sun, so people leave snow-

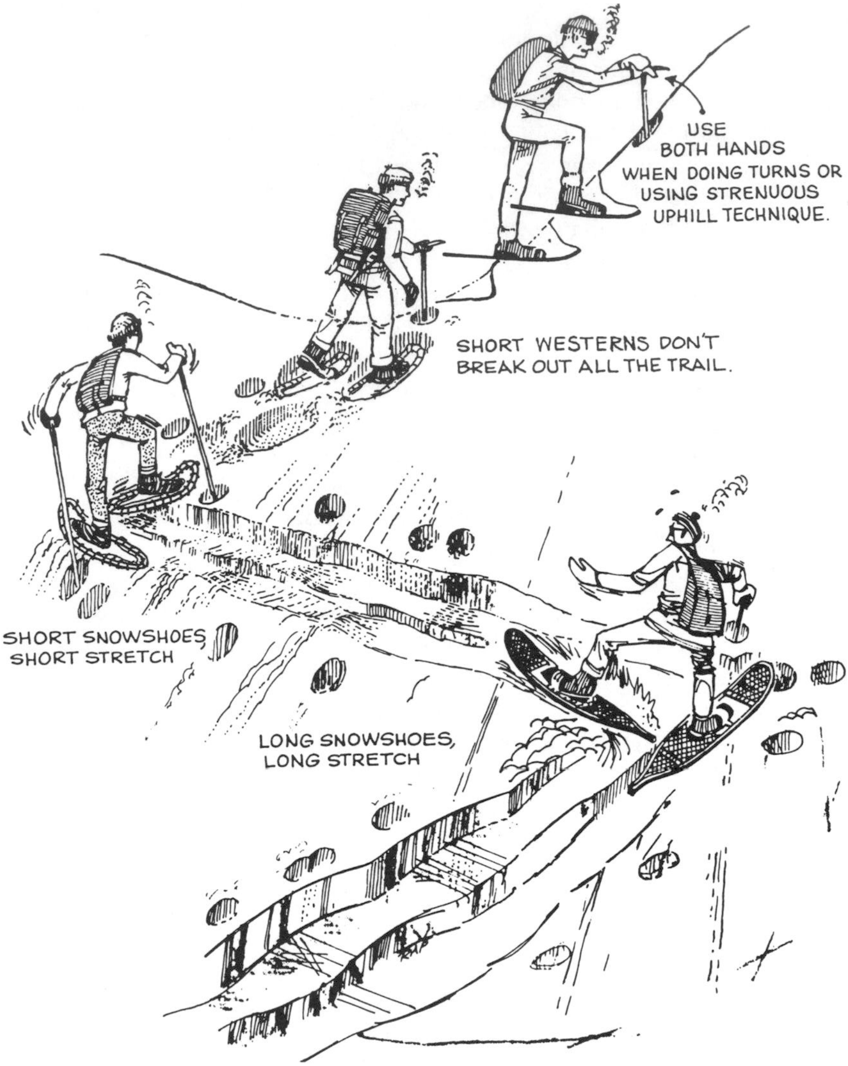

Fig. 20. Making switchback turns and, at top, toeing straight in on steep pitch

shoes and kick steps in the snow to the summit. Sometimes crampons are handy, too, if an unusually hard crust has developed.

This is the pattern that has developed in the West since World War II. Probably part of the switchback tradition was aided by the 10 × 56-inch Yukon snowshoes that were so available after the war. The price was right, and if you couldn't find the regular trail everyone understood about switchbacking; the narrow Yukons were good for traversing, but you certainly can't kick steps straight up with those high toes. It is interesting to speculate on what might have happened if any of those flat-toe, super-step-kicking eastern snowshoes or snowshoers had been around to teach us westerners how it's done.

However, the 12-inch-wide eastern step-kicking beavertails had problems on a narrow western traverse and made the 10-inch-wide Yukons look good. A narrow width makes it possible to edge the snowshoe in three to four inches and continue to climb comfortably. Edging can be simply kicking the snowshoe sideways into the slope (Figure 21), or moving the boot heel as far toward the uphill side of the slope as possible, then stamping down and forcing the edge of the snowshoe into the slope.

Fig. 21. Edging with narrow Western snowshoes in snow that is firm but not crusted

In the late 1960s I further modified a 10 × 36-inch modified bearpaw by moving the hinge and binding far forward. This provided the prototype for the present Western snowshoes: it created a shoe that was narrow for traversing and also had a flat toe for excellent step kicking. Today's tiny Western models are used as an extension of bare-boot climbing on firm spring snow: the extra flotation provided by the snowshoe makes this early spring climbing possible in January or February rather than May.

The typical Western snowshoe as it eventually evolved has a high toe, three to five inches. Western step-kicking technique requires soft snow, but instead of kicking through a crust the snowshoe is more often stomped down to pack a step (Figure 22). Frequently switchbacks are nearly straight up the slope rather than the gentle angle shown in Figure 20.

The high toe works well in two situations. First, it is easier to pull up out of deep, soft snow when ascending a slope, because it rides up rather than burrowing under as a flat toe does. And second, it also pulls out of deep snow when descending by plunge stepping or simply walking on the level. The high toe kicks steps adequately in soft western snow, although the flat toe is much better in an eastern crust. Generally, western snow

Fig. 22. Step-kicking in soft snow with Western snowshoe

is softer than the crusted snow in the East, so the high toe is preferred in the West.

Snowshoers in British Columbia use the same western switchback technique, but their soft powder snow dictates a larger snowshoe. A 9×38-inch Western and the 10×36-inch Green Mountain with forward-mounted binding are large enough to give adequate flotation, yet short enough to be maneuverable and still kick steps. Frequently a smaller snowshoe would be large enough, but there is the hoar frost around boulders, stumps, and any other object sticking up in the snow. Cold temperatures create this zone of unstructured crystals around these objects. This may be to B.C. what spruce traps are to New England: the three-foot-long snowshoe is the minimum length to keep from falling into the hoar. In May when the snow gets firmer, smaller snowshoes are more practical.

Some suggestions on switchbacks and step kicking may be of help to beginners who are unfamiliar with these techniques. Usually ascend at a grade a little less than the maximum angle the snowshoes will climb (the maximum angle of course requires that you hang on with great effort, always on the verge of slipping, and is very tiring). Use an angle of ascent that is comfortable and lets you relax somewhat. At the point of turning, for example to the right, plant the left snowshoe firmly and stamp it in so it will hold. If you are using an ice axe, place it in the slope above the binding of the left snowshoe and work it in securely. Ski poles should be planted below the snowshoes, alongside the boot heels. Then shift weight to the left snowshoe and axe or poles, face the slope, and swing the right snowshoe around to point it in the direction the next switchback will take, and shove it into the snow.

Make sure you place it so the tail is not on the left snowshoe. Stamp the right web into the snow and gently shift weight and step on it. Try to stay well above your previous trail, which has undermined the snow you are now building the turn on. Reverse the procedure for a left turn (Figure 20).

The very short, narrow aluminum-frame snowshoes allow a modified technique. The 8×25-inch model, for example, requires merely that you kick steps as for snow climbing without snowshoes. These webs are so small that they do not interfere seriously with placing your feet on turns.

As each succeeding snowshoer uses the turn the trail shoulders may slough off and latecomers may have a harder time getting around than the leader. By all means use special care in placing snowshoes precisely where they were placed before, widening and deepening the tracks for those who follow. Special care in placing snowshoes, axe, or poles will pay dividends in avoiding slips. Sometimes there is only one way past an obstacle. Be sure to preserve the trail so others following do not have to rebuild it.

There are other ways to make the snowshoe turn easier. Plan to use the gentlest places on a slope for the turns; look ahead and pick the route to use the terrain to your advantage. Avoid the steepest parts and don't hesitate to make short switchbacks between main turns. Use trees and their branches for handholds. When the snow is soft enough, the trail can be

Fig. 23. Traversing with large snowshoe usually develops two trails, one above the other.

Fig. 24. Short snowshoes allow a single-file traverse.

two snowshoe widths wide and relatively level, but often the snow is too firm for that and requires one snowshoe trail slightly above the other (Figure 23). People on 36-inch and shorter snowshoes have an advantage in this situation as these short snowshoes may be placed one ahead of the other. This keeps the feet at the same height (Figure 24) which is less tiring than the two-trail technique. Beavertails overlap some and can be used almost single file, but still are at a disadvantage compared to the eight-inch width on sidehills.

Balance is critical when placing one snowshoe ahead of the other. Ordinarily the feet are spaced far enough apart for good stability. But traversing with the snowshoes single file decreases stability, so the poles or axe must compensate. A person with short snowshoes may save some effort on a traverse, but at the expense of irritating someone in the group who is wearing long Yukons.

Another benefit of using short snowshoes with forward-mounted bindings is their practicality for kicking the toes in and climbing straight up a steep pitch (step kicking). As this technique is strenuous and requires soft snow, it is limited to short pitches. Long slopes with enough soft snow to kick the toes in for a good step could also be steep and unstable enough to avalanche (see chapter 10). The method is to swing the snowshoe backward and flip the tail up. The toe is kicked straight into the slope, with the web horizontal and the tails sticking out in the air. The forward-hinged 36-inchers and shorter shoes work well for this; a strong snowshoer can use 10 × 46-inchers, too, although it is more difficult. Obviously the snow must be right—soft enough to kick the snowshoe in 12 to 16 inches and still firm enough to support the snowshoer.

Long steps, spaced wider apart laterally, are necessary, as the lower step, deep as it needs to be, badly undermines the step above. Steps such as these are weak and do not form a trail adequate for a large party. The main use of this technique is along ridges where drifting creates slopes too steep to angle up and without enough room to switchback around the obstruction. With more skill and practice you will find other places where a short, steep pitch climbed straight up may save time. Although admittedly of limited use, this technique is one more way to save energy over a long pull.

Techniques such as the kick turn and toeing in straight up are easier if you can extend your legs and take long steps, placing the forward snowshoe in undisturbed snow that has not been undermined by other steps. Movements must be smooth and precise, which may be a little too much for the untrained muscles of beginners, who experience "sewing machine leg" when fatigue begins to build up and overextended muscles begin to protest. Muscle spasms cause a jerking that probably precedes a real cramp.

The eastern step-kicking technique was developed for eastern conditions, which included crusted snow, steep slopes, dense forests, and local trail habits. Snowfall in the White Mountains of New Hampshire is about half the average in the Cascades. The January—or December or February—thaws are caused by moist air from the Atlantic or Gulf of Mexico moving inland, pushing cold air out and dumping rain in this normally frigid area.

Rain on the cold snow may not penetrate more than an inch or two. Arctic air from Canada immediately repossesses the land, and the return to zero guarantees a quick-frozen hard crust. Often there is powder snow underneath. The crust is too hard to edge a snowshoe into, too weak to bare-boot it, so when it gets too steep to snowshoe-crampon up it, you sink the ice axe in for stability and start driving the toes of your snowshoes through it (Figure 25). And hope you don't splinter the toe of your snowshoe frame against a granite stone just under the surface.

Occasionally Alaskan climbers get pinned down in a camp near Denali Pass above 18,000 feet on Mt. McKinley and report wind of "at least" 100 mph. They don't really have it so tough, however. In New England it is normal to have temperatures of –5° or –10°F on summits, with a 35-mph wind; it is fairly common to register velocities over 80 mph. The world record wind velocity was measured in New Hampshire on Mt. Washington's 6288-foot summit at 231 mph in 1934. Winds over 100 mph are recorded frequently, often at subzero temperatures.

Fig. 25. Eastern step-kicking in crust

Westerners have difficulty comprehending that the kind of weather they experience above 10,000 feet and take several days to get to may be suffered on a day trip in eastern mountains at 5000 feet! In spite of the East's extremely severe climate, snowshoers swarm up these peaks all winter. Difficulty of travel that would limit western snowshoers to a trickle seems to incite the locals.

As you travel more on snow it will become apparent that patience is necessary to enjoy winter travel. You can't race in, see the view, and sprint out; it's too difficult to move fast on snow. Also, during the winter months there are fewer daylight hours. Take time to enjoy the trip—make the scenery along the way as much a goal as the destination is. Patience also means not getting upset by minor equipment problems and changes of plan. A broken strap or loose rivet is never convenient to repair, but it should be fixed before it becomes major breakage. Be sure to get camp set up in time to get adequate rest. Realize that snow is inconsistent and revise your schedule if necessary. Take time to avoid possible avalanche areas (see chapter 10). Do a good job of routefinding, trail-breaking, and camping, and if necessary give up an objective if the danger from storm or avalanche is too great. The penalty for error in the winter is much greater than it is in the summer.

CHAPTER 8

Snow Conditions

Snow is at all times sensitive to an infinite variety of modifying conditions. The only predictable thing about it is that it will be different higher up, around the corner, or over the ridge. Temperature and wind are the determining factors. Cold temperatures are associated with powder snow. A crusted condition results from changing temperatures: warming and thawing melt the surface, then cold temperatures freeze it. The areas that have warmed the most will refreeze, pack, and become the most firm. Generally the temperature is colder at higher elevations, dropping approximately 3°F with each additional thousand feet.

North sides of mountains, deep, shaded valleys with heavy timber, and lee slopes that collect windblown snow are the slowest to firm up. North sides of mountains and lee slopes also have the hazard of avalanches the longest.

Wind does two things. It packs and therefore firms areas where it blows constantly. Wind pack has the same effect on powder snow as increased temperature and is an advantage to winter travel. Snow falling in wind usually forms wind slab, an adverse effect of wind that will be discussed more fully with avalanches. Wind slab can be on lee slopes, where much windblown snow has drifted in, or on areas that face the wind if the new snow is not packed and consolidated with the underlying snowpack. Either circumstance may form an extremely unstable condition.

The force of gravity is another factor modifying the behavior of snow on slopes of mountains or hills. A fresh, stable deposit of snow, when sufficiently warmed by the sun, may begin to flow like water and avalanche into the valley bottom. Or the wind may blow certain areas free of snow, depositing it in extra deep layers in sheltered locations.

The textbook set of snow conditions in the Cascades is slush in the valley bottoms with powder snow on the upper slopes and variations of both between. However, conditions seldom follow the pattern exactly because forest, cloud cover, wind, and direction of slopes create microclimates.

For example, a fresh snowfall may remain powdery until storm clouds pass and the sun comes out. Then sheltered open south slopes may become slushy from valley floor to ridgetop on a warm afternoon, freezing at night into an iron-hard crust. A thick stand of tall evergreens just above the valley bottom may shelter powder snow for several days after the storm has passed and temperatures have warmed, yet snow melting off the trees may refreeze under each tree into an icy patch surrounded by powder. North slopes may not warm up for weeks at a time, and so have deep powder most of the winter. Ridgetops cooled by constant wind do not develop crust, yet may be wind-packed hard as ice. Nearby may be a patch of powder cooled by the wind, yet on the side facing the sun, or there may be slush on the lee side of a clump of trees, sheltered from the wind and warmed by the sun.

Knowledge of local conditions and routes that are avalanche-free is very important. Sometimes cold temperatures, powder snow, and the short daylight hours of January and early February effectively limit snow travel to foothills and nearby destinations. With firmer snow and longer days later in winter, you can get to the lower viewpoints in a few hours and more distant peaks are reasonable objectives.

Colder mountain ranges do not experience the cycle of new snowfall/warming and settling/new snow/warming as often as the Cascades, which have a marine climate. Some generalizations may be made on snow condition and temperature pattern. No generalizations about *specific* avalanche hazard in a given area can be made. Avalanche hazard must be determined in the field, at each location, in person (see chapter 10).

The Rocky Mountains of both the United States and Canada, the Interior Ranges of British Columbia, the Wasatch in Utah, and the Sierra have certain similarities due to their cold temperatures. Mid December to mid or late January frequently see the record minimum temperatures. There are usually several feet of snow on the ground by this time. Severe subzero Fahrenheit readings cause depth hoar buildup within or at the bottom of the snowpack, which creates a great avalanche hazard. (Depth hoar is discussed in chapter 10.)

Powder snow in these ranges generally lasts from mid November to varying dates from mid February to mid April. This depends on weather patterns as spring arrives earlier some years than others. In these mountain areas the favorite snowshoes are the 9 × 38-inch Western or 10 × 36-inch with forward-mounted binding, because hikers generally avoid the period—the first few days after snowfalls—in which larger models would be needed. This is due to the extreme avalanche hazard during and after snowfalls, which often can be several feet per storm. Hikers and climbers in these rugged mountain areas must have firm snow for safety and reasonable traveling conditions. Later in spring, when the snow is really firm, some backpackers use as small as 9 × 30 and 8 × 25 Western.

In the Anchorage, Alaska, area the 9 × 38-inch or 10 × 36-inch is a little small some winters since heavy snowfall and cold temperatures prolong deep powder snow. In the Interior, such as Big Delta, a 14 × 48-inch beavertail can sink more than knee deep. Sled dog racers on the Anchorage to Nome 1200-mile Iditarod race may want even larger models when bucking deep powder.

The Wyoming/Montana areas are regarded by the locals as the coldest in the lower 48 states, with a record low of –63°F in the high-elevation Jackson Hole/Yellowstone plateau area. The coldest period is during late December to mid January. Snow is powder, with not much before Christmas; storms build it deeper without much base until late winter. Depth hoar formation is extensive. By March the snow is firm for good traveling. The 6000-foot-high valleys in this area record the lowest minimums, but also warm up the fastest in the spring and on bright sunny days.

Heaviest snowfall is on the west side of the Tetons, Wind Rivers, and the many ranges in Montana and Idaho. Most of the storms that drop snow in the western ranges originate on the Pacific Ocean. Heavy snowfall with wind is common and creates severe slab avalanche hazard extensively during the winter.

The Rockies and other ranges of Colorado have a somewhat similar overall pattern of snow conditions and weather. The coldest temperatures are usually the last week of December and early January. Depth hoar formation is extensive. Despite these conditions there is a strong snowshoeing tradition in the north Colorado Rockies. Deep powder persists in sheltered and forested areas. Large areas above timber line are usually firmer. When avalanche danger is high, activity shifts to lesser peaks (there are 130 peaks over 11,000 feet in Colorado). Wooden snowshoes 12 × 28 inches to 10 × 36 inches are used, as well as 9 × 38-inch and 9 × 30-inch Westerns.

The more southern areas of the snowbelt, such as in Colorado and to the south, experience much more sun and clear weather in late winter, which tends to firm up the snow, especially on south-facing slopes in these high, cold ranges.

Late winter does not see an end to heavy storm, as March and April normally have heavy snowfall with wind. By late spring—April or so—there may be a crust on the snow in places, so you can bareboot it. The San Juans in southwest Colorado and the western side of these mountains probably have the heaviest snowfall. Near Wolf Creek Pass in south Colorado, low temperatures can reach –50°F.

The Wasatch have somewhat the same snow conditions as the Rockies. Cold weather begins in late October or November. There is usually snow in the mountains when temperatures reach the lowest minimums in late December and January, with –20°F to be expected and the record around –35°F. These temperatures and heavy snowfall guarantee lots of powder snow through the winter. Snowfall is usually accompanied by wind with lots of slab avalanche hazard.

There may not be as strong a tradition of snowshoeing in the Wasatch as other places in the United States. The Yukon and plastic snowshoes are more in evidence in the gentler mountains north of Salt Lake. Some people feel it's too cold until mid-February, and snow travel is easier on firmer snow later in the winter. The valley elevation is 4500 feet; smaller summits are 8000 feet, where there are avalanche-free routes.

The main Wasatch, with summits around 12,000 feet, are rather strenuous for the casual snowshoer and more in the class of the Tetons for winter ascents. Clear weather and bright sunshine make daytime temperatures considerably above nighttime lows. By April conditions may be changing from winter to spring, especially on south-facing slopes.

The Sierra Nevada have some similarities to the other high ranges mentioned, in that winter normally brings powder snow in generous amounts. Subzero temperatures cause formation of depth hoar, with its long-term avalanche hazard. The coldest temperatures are in the high, over-6000-foot part of northern Owens Valley around Bridgeport.

There are drought years with little snow, but December, January, and February are the traditional time of deep powder. Snow falls with wind, so the steep slopes are most dangerous. In late winter and spring there are probably longer intervals between storms.

This range is much farther south than the Montana Rockies, so clear days without wind can bring some thawing and freezing to firm up snow. However, the heaviest snowfall may occur in March, April, and May, which causes a spring snow avalanche hazard in addition to the depth hoar problem.

Mid February may see firm snow for good travel on lower mountains, with avalanche-free routes. March and April may see good conditions on the higher peaks, but this depends entirely on the weather pattern of the year, as the snowfall pattern is so changeable from one year to the next. Snowshoes may be used through May in places. The change from summer to winter is one of the greatest hazards. Hikers who are accustomed to the extreme summer heat often get caught by winter temperatures and snowfall, which may occur as early as September or October or not until November or December.

The San Gabriels, San Bernardino, and San Jacinto mountains south of the Sierra also have snowshoeing and touring. These summits of 10,000 feet to 11,500 feet have all the hazards of more northern mountains. Powder snow firms up more rapidly but there are subzero temperatures at high elevations and avalanche hazard is present. The smaller Western snowshoes are becoming the favorites in both the Sierra and the San Gabriels.

Large snowshoes such as the 11 × 57-inch Cree or Ojibway are the favorite for gentler terrain west of the Great Lakes. There is lots of powder snow because of the normal subfreezing and subzero temperatures all winter, until mid March or so.

From the Minneapolis-St. Paul area north to the iron ranges at Hibbing there is deep powder plus wind. The record minimum of –47°F and wind means extreme cold for winter campers. Open areas and lakes do wind pack and make for easier traveling in this area. North of the iron ranges there is less wind, and in these areas snow may remain dry and powdery all winter. Conditions vary tremendously and sometimes a crust will form. Northern Wisconsin and the Upper Peninsula of Michigan can expect deep snow, six to eight feet, so until the snow firms up in this area the large snowshoes still are number one.

In the East, expect powder snow with no base by New Year's Day. More snowfalls of powder followed by a thaw and refreezing puts icy layers in the snowpack, with powder in between. High winds above tree line sweep any snowfall to lee sides, causing avalanche hazard. Numerous of the slides—for example, Jefferson Slide, Adams Slide and the more publicized Tuckerman and Huntington ravines on Mt. Washington—frequently avalanche. Rime ice build-up creates a need for boot crampons above tree line. There is a similarity between terrain above tree line in the East and the last 500 feet of Mt. Rainier, which is also subject to rime ice build-up called sastrugi. A cloud cap on Rainier indicates high winds inside the cap. The same is true in New Hampshire; clouds on the ridges indicate high winds above tree line. After the sap starts running in March the snow gets slushy on the lower elevations and it's time to start rock climbing.

To meet the great variety of conditions found in the mountains, you need to know which snowshoe works best on varied terrain (see chapter 1). Don't be tempted to get a Yukon on the theory that deep snow is the only problem in the mountains. First of all, the snowshoe must be used on sidehills, making narrow width of prime importance. When more than two feet of snow falls, the trail ledge on sidehills begins to disappear. On the level, three or four feet will hide blazes on trees; six to eight feet will be above the limbless section of trailside trees. Even sections of road drift over and develop formidable slopes that descend steeply to valley floor in midwinter. If an otherwise simple route crosses a creek and there are four feet or more of snow on the ground, it will be a struggle to get down one side and up the other unless you have a shovel and snowshoes designed and equipped to climb well. Trees on sidehills have deep wells—holes in the snow around the trunks—that must be detoured around, perhaps on steep slopes. Fallen trees and drifts on gentle sidehills can create short, steep slopes on otherwise easy hikes. And the mountaineer on the ridgetops is often following a narrow path beside cornices and over drifts.

An eight-inch-wide snowshoe can be edged if the snow is

not too hard, but not nearly as effectively as a climbing boot or ski. Wider snowshoes of course are just that much less effective. Bindings are too flexible to really "hammer" even narrow snowshoes into hard snow on a sidehill. The nearly straight frames on some models hold better than the curving sides of the bearpaw and beavertail.

Long spells of subzero temperature will freeze even fast-moving mountain streams. This can be a real help by eliminating the problems of crossing unbridged streams. A solidly frozen stream can sometimes shorten a route that has a long trail approach or can eliminate some bushwhacking. However, be extremely careful when crossing any stream on ice, as it frequently is anything but solid and is full of air pockets.

At subzero temperatures flowing water may freeze and block the channel. The water may find a different route under snow. There often is water on top of the ice in a lake solidly frozen. Look for depressions in the snow around the edges of a lake as these may indicate a spring flowing into the lake, creating thin ice at that spot. Falling into water at zero temperatures is quite dangerous so check thickness of ice before walking out on a frozen stream or lake.

There isn't space to describe all the possible weather patterns and snow conditions in all the snowshoeing areas in the United States and Canada. Reading about it here won't guarantee that you will recognize the dangers described when you are actually in an area new to you. The best this information can do is point out that an outing in a different place can really be great, but you should get some local expert to advise you—and help you realize that equipment perfect in one area may not be so great elsewhere.

CHAPTER 9

Routefinding

A glistening snow cover mantling the winter landscape is a thing of magic, giving mountain and hill country such an allure that more and more people each year are drawn to explore its beauty. However, reaching a goal presents an unaccustomed problem in winter. In summer, even distant backcountry can be reached by trails, since the main problem in trail routefinding is choosing the proper fork at junctions. Storm and bad weather have relatively little effect on this type of routefinding, and maps and trail guides are usually adequate reference material.

Deep snow changes all this by covering not only the trail, but also trail signs, blazes on trees, and even trailside shelters. In heavy timber there is frequently a lane through the trees, but in more open country all trail signs disappear. In places exposed to wind and drifting snow, such obvious features as roads disappear altogether. Ridgetops are changed the most—drifts 20 or 30 feet high alter the visual aspect of the landscape and knolls may appear where gullies were in the summer. Some of these changes are for the better, as a great deal of brush and garbage is buried and some gullies are filled with snow, leveling out a depression or making easy creek crossings where wading was required in summer.

The snowshoer's problem is similar to that of the summer backcountry traveler who goes beyond the trails: a route is chosen through obstacles such as cliffs, stream gorges, and impassible thickets, but rather than routefinding by trail junctions, the snowshoer is looking for topographical features such as the places where two streams or canyons meet and is relying on

Climbing above valley fog in Washington's eastern Cascades

other landmarks instead of counting mileposts.

A major problem with this method is identifying side canyons or tributary streams. Questions arise as to whether the side canyon you are looking at is the one shown on the map. It is difficult visualizing terrain by interpreting the convoluted contour lines on a map. Frequently trees will totally hide a very obvious tributary stream or valley.

In rugged mountain terrain with high ridges and deep valleys routefinding is fairly simple. It is obvious when a ridge is crossed. There is, however, a lot of travel through forested country where major peaks are hidden by trees or winter clouds—or where, as in the Midwest, there are no peaks. Many winter travelers are familiar with the country; they follow compass courses in summer and plan to do the same in winter. Competent navigation by map and compass has certain advantages over using visual points of reference. For one thing, the compass doesn't require clear weather to operate accurately.

Rather than go into a detailed course in orienteering here, I will use the simplest, most basic method of setting and following a compass course to a single objective.

Place the section of map you are using on a level spot, such as a pack without magnetic items inside it—camera, knife, etc.—with the compass on it. When the compass needle stops swinging, align the north-south grid lines of the map with north on the compass. Plot your course on the map. As you travel, you can then use magnetic north without adjusting for the local declination.

Select an objective or point to be reached on the map—for instance a stream junction a mile or so away. A direct line across the center of the compass to that point on the map should provide a true bearing to follow. With the map removed, but with the compass oriented as before, sight across the compass at the same reading. The stream junction will be out that direction—a mile or so away.

If you are traveling alone, pick an easily identifiable object along the intended path and proceed to that point. If you are part of a group, send a person to the farthest point you can see on that line, and when he is at that point sight to make sure he is still on the compass line. This person then uses his compass to align the next person on the next most distant visible point, and so on.

To check on the distance traveled, allow 34 steps of average length on the level for a distance of 100 feet. Use fewer steps for long steps downhill and more for short steps uphill. Measure the mileage on the map and make an approximation by tallying the distance between sightings with the compass. This must be written down, since there are about 53 hundred-foot sightings at the 34-step average in a mile, or 1802 strides.

Another method of checking distance traveled is to use your watch for elapsed time and estimated speed. At a speed of four miles an hour, it will take 15 minutes to go one mile. Faster or slower speeds can be figured from this easily remembered number.

Be sure that following a compass course is appropriate to the terrain. Steep mountain country with deep canyons or ravines and high ridges is not the best place to set a compass course direct to the objective. In leveler country it is easier to go directly across streams and divides. In steeper country it may be more appropriate to set a compass course through thick timber to a place, for example, where a valley has some gentle slopes to climb to cross a ridge. A course change would be necessary when reaching the point to start up the side of the ridge. At the ridgetop, it might be necessary to set a course into the next valley, perhaps toward a good stream crossing. It takes practice to follow a compass course rapidly and accurately.

For more information along this line, check the navigation section of *Mountaineering: The Freedom of the Hills* or some references on orienteering. Some skill in navigation techniques is essential when traveling by compass in forested and rugged backcountry.

Although it is desirable to be able to see where you are going, especially in new country, it is best to be so familiar with the area that you are able to recognize small landmarks if the weather is cloudy and major landmarks are hidden. The key to this is preparation. Choose winter objectives you have been to in summer, or make certain there is someone in the group who knows the area. Not all trail signs are hidden, but it takes an observant person to discern a blaze on a tree down in a hole where sheltering branches have created a depression in the snow around the trunk, or a limb that has obviously been chopped or sawed off, or a section of Forest Service phone line almost hidden in the snow. Study the summer trails and note their location in regard to features that will show clearly in winter, so that if you lose a trail you can continue and pick it up farther along.

One danger in mountain country is potential avalanche slopes or chutes. The new 15-minute (1 inch equals about 1 mile) U.S. Geological Survey quad maps that show forest cover give a hint of possible locations of avalanches, such as contour lines that indicate a steep slope in an area without forest cover. The 7½-minute series is even more helpful. U.S. Forest Service maps are of no help in this, nor do summer hiking and climbing guides generally provide such information, and some summer trails cross or ascend slopes that frequently avalanche in winter. Observe the route carefully for avalanche chutes, recognizable as gullies swept clear of trees and leading unobstructed from valley floor to ridgetop snowfields. Stay out of these potential funnels for the snow above may be unstable and avalanche down the gully, and do not hesitate to change your planned route from an open gully to a forested slope. If you snowshoe in areas where avalanches are possible, you should learn the danger signs (see chapter 10).

The easy part of routefinding is getting to the objective—a viewpoint, a mountaintop, or a snow-covered meadow beside a stream. Like summer hikers, snowshoers are inclined to relax when following the return trail, and indeed it is usually as obvious as a summer trail. But in windswept areas, take extra precautions, for a change in weather can create conditions that make returning extremely difficult unless the route is marked by brightly colored plastic flagging tied on trees, or by bamboo wands (garden stakes two or three feet long with flagging attached) that may be carried along and placed in open treeless areas. Flags and wands should be picked up on return and carried out. It may be hard to be serious about marking what in clear weather is an obvious route, but clouds and storms can eliminate even a prominent set of tracks and obscure the landscape so that each clump of trees, each ridge or draw looks exactly like every other one. On a clear day the snowshoe trail appears as a slash across each open spot, but a few minutes of blowing snow can obliterate it. In cloudy conditions even flagging and wands are not too effective unless they are very close together or you have recorded compass bearings for the return trail. Even the huge cairns marking trails on Mt. Washington in New Hampshire are hard to find in a white-out, a condition that occurs when clouds merge with blowing snow and all land-

New snow is one sign of potential avalanche hazards.

marks are hidden.

The simplest method of taking a compass bearing back down the trail for your return is as follows: face in the direction you will be traveling, place the compass a safe distance from any magnetic object such as exposure meter, watch, ice axe, etc., (a good place is on your mittens laid on the snow) and let the needle stop swinging. Line up north on the compass with the north end of the needle. Sight across the compass from the point where you are toward the direction you will want to return. Record this figure.

This is all that an amateur needs to know to get across an unmarked area where visibility is poor. Greater expertise is required if there are long distances to travel by compass and changes in direction are necessary at places where there are no identifying features, but the procedure is the same. On the return, set the compass out, let the needle stop swinging, and set north on the dial to the north end of the needle. Walk in the direction your notes indicate, trying to keep on the proper heading, and you should arrive at the next known point without difficulty.

This knowledge is a real safeguard in high open country

above timber line. Frequently the snow is so firm no real snowshoe tracks are left. If clouds move in, and a little snow blows into what tracks there are, a white-out occurs. The effect can be so complete it is hard to tell where the surface is until your snowshoe actually touches it. A white-out can be very confusing even on a small open area, but if you can travel from known point to known point by compass you are well prepared for the task. The same problem exists in gentle, low-elevation country. Crossing large frozen lakes in poor visibility requires a compass.

The most difficult routefinding is in featureless, rolling country such as the foothills on the fringes of the mountain ranges. In gentle country you can be on or near a divide and cross into another stream valley without realizing it, then follow it down away from the starting point.

The compass is of little help unless you are at a known point and want to get to another known point. To find your way cross-country without a trail, where there are no visible landmarks, you must prepare the information such as compass bearings on the way in to have the accurate information necessary to get out in a storm.

Snowshoers are getting farther into the mountains each winter. In addition to the increased avalanche danger from heavy snowfall in steep country, a new challenge is being accepted in winter glacier travel. Routefinding is the same on a glacier, winter or summer. Note the crevasses, some of which remain open all winter, and pick a route around them as you would in summer. The hollows are usually safer because the glacier surface is under compression and crevasses seldom occur there. Areas where the surface is shoved up, as a large mound a quarter mile or so across, generally are crevassed heavily, since the surface is under tension.

In winter there is much less indication of crevasses than in summer, when there is no snowfall and warm temperatures cause faster glacier movement. Unless the distance and depth are very great, windblown snow may bridge even wide crevasses by the same process that builds snow cornices out 10 to 20 feet on the lee side of ridges. When the cornice does bridge the crevasse, the snow drifts on across and leaves no clue that a few feet down there is unsupported snow. It is doubtful that any but small crevasses fill completely with windblown snow and there are many holes under the apparently innocent, smooth glacier in winter and summer. One additional problem in winter is that it is difficult to locate crevasses by probing with the ice axe. The snow is so soft everywhere that plunging the shaft in to the head does not necessarily indicate a crevasse underneath.

Snowshoes decrease the chance of stepping through a weak snow bridge by distributing the weight over a large area. It is likely that only a very wide, weak bridge would collapse under a person wearing footgear three feet long. However, in winter as in summer, keep the party roped up.

Crevasse rescue on snowshoes is the same as with crampons, except that the person being rescued places the boot heel, rather than the toe, in the slings (unless one can remove snowshoes while hanging from the climbing rope without losing them down the crevasse). As in summer, ice axes must be used for belays (the ice axe basket must be removed for this, so be sure it is quickly detachable). Raising techniques are described in *Mountaineering: The Freedom of the Hills*. Study the techniques before going into crevassed terrain.

Cold temperatures slow down the movement of glaciers. However, icefalls are active all winter, so choose your route, as you would in summer, to minimize dangers of seracs falling on the climbing party. It is surprising how many blocks tumble down icefalls at night in zero temperature. But major activity is in the morning after sunlight hits the ice and warms it, however slightly, and after sundown when the chill begins to freeze the ice a little harder. And anytime in between when the glacier feels like it.

In summary, there are several things for beginning snowshoers to remember: First, be familiar with the area you are in. Second, follow a trail if possible. Third, when the trail is obscured by snow, pick a route that avoids dangers and obstructions and is guided by prominent landmarks. Fourth, mark the return trail with flagging or wands in case it storms and landmarks are not visible for the return; carry a map and compass and correlate them with your route. Fifth, have a plan for survival if you must stay overnight or longer and wait out a storm.

These rules are not fun and games—there simply isn't enough dumb luck to supply all who need it.

CHAPTER 10

Winter Safety

Many of the objective hazards of winter travel cannot be predicted with any great degree of accuracy but must be observed and evaluated. It is possible to say a particular slope is prone to avalanche, or that large globs of snow fall off trees after heavy storms; but on-the-spot judgments of the immediate danger must be made in each particular case. The hazards described here should convince you of the necessity of leaving a detailed itinerary with friends before your trip.

Lakes and Streams

Snow travelers occasionally fall through the ice covering a stream or lake. Lakes may have two or three feet of ice on them and still have some hazards. The main one, aside from insufficient ice to walk on safely, is a spring that enters the lake. The relatively warmer water will melt the ice—or prevent the spot from freezing—which causes a weak spot. Note places along the margin of the lake where snow depth is less. These may indicate such a spring.

Snowshoers crossing lakes that have many inches of ice sometimes wade into slush on top of the ice, even on subzero days. This may be water from a stream that has frozen at the shore but continues to seep a small amount of water on top of the ice under an insulating layer of snow. This does not necessarily indicate weak and dangerous ice.

Some people feel that a great weight of snow on a solidly frozen over lake will crack the ice and permit water to well up, causing a weak area better not used for a snowshoe hike. (In

Winter snowshoe ascent of Mount Daniel in the Washington Cascades

the Cascades there may be no ice on a lake; what appears to be a lake with thick ice and a snow cover is in reality several feet of snow floating on the lake with no ice at all.)

Another cause of weak ice sounds like the spruce-trap dwarfs of the East but is more likely to be fatal. Large carp, perhaps to 50 pounds apiece, abound in some Midwest lakes. They may congregate in schools of several hundred, feeding in a particular inlet. If you fall through thin ice and get trampled by a herd of these startled, stampeding fish, you may feel that they were somehow to blame. You could be right. It might be that the carp were gathered at a spot with lots of good feed where a spring ran into the lake, and the warmer spring water created thin ice. Or perhaps so many large fish in a small area created enough turbulence to slow formation of the ice. According to the natives, however, sheer body warmth melts the ice. You may take your pick of reasons while climbing out of the hole you fell through.

Generally mountain streams flow too fast to freeze into good access routes. The main problem is that they are open and deep all winter. Eight to ten feet of snow on either bank makes them as formidable as a crevasse in a glacier. If there isn't a bridge or a foot log, the hike may necessarily end at the stream crossing. Even when there is a bridge, it may be dangerous to cross. Walking on a narrow ridge of snow eight feet above the bridge decking and even farther above the streambed calls for flawless technique: side-step across very gently, keeping the feet directly over the bridge. If you are using a footlog, it may be safer to clear the snow off, although this may expose frozen and icy bark. Side-stepping may leave snowshoe tails and toes hanging out in the air if the log is narrow, a frightening view for some.

Instep crampons with one-inch-long steel spikes attached to the snowshoes give the greatest security on slippery footlogs and icy stones in streams, biting into these surfaces much better than any rubber-soled boot. If the water is deep, unhook one shoulder strap and the waistband of your pack to make it easier to jettison in case of a fall into the water. If a rope is available, it is a good idea to rope up, or rig a hand line for safety on dangerous stream crossings. It may not be possible to stop someone from landing in the creek, but the rope will ensure getting out.

When there is no log or bridge, or where one is impassible, it may be possible to dig a trail down the snow wall on one side of the stream, step across, and dig a ramp up the wall on the other side. Be careful to keep your snowshoes out of the water if traveling in powder snow, for several pounds of powder will freeze on wet snowshoes in the first steps, unless they happen to be plastic. Cross streams that are frozen over or bridged with snow with extreme caution, especially if the water underneath is deeper than your boot tops.

Use all necessary precautions to avoid getting in the water. Other party members should be ready with ice axes, rope, or handy poles to provide firmly anchored handholds to help any unfortunate snowshoer back out if the ice breaks. It's hard to pull your snowshoes out of a mass of slush and ice chunks, and also very unpleasant to reach bare hands down in the frigid mass to unbuckle bindings to make a less encumbered exit from the icy stream.

Idiot Makers

Part of the attraction of winter is walking among snow-covered trees—they can be even more lovely than in summer. At times they are covered so deeply that no green shows, and the top or a high branch may have an accumulation of snow weighing many pounds. Periodically these huge bombs—called idiot makers where I come from—fall out of trees a hundred or more feet tall, landing with a "whoomp" and making an impact crater in the snow. I know of no one who has been injured by one, but from personal experience, I know they can knock you flat. Keep a wary eye open when the trees are carrying heavy loads of snow in their tops; wearing a hard hat isn't too bad an idea in this situation.

These treetop globs of snow are a phenomenon of heavy snow country where the snow falls softly and silently without wind. At higher elevations, especially on ridgetops, trees appear to be completely covered with snow. This is usually rime ice, which is formed when wind-driven mist freezes on trees or rocks upon contact. (A tap with your hand will indicate that the rime is anything but soft.)

White-Outs

In conditions of dense fog, cloud, and often blowing snow there may be no visual clues to location. Sky and snow merge and the horizon disappears and it is difficult to tell whether you are walking uphill or downhill. Until you touch it with an axe, pole, or snowshoe, it is impossible to tell where the surface is. Frequently people walk off drifts and tumble because they simply cannot see the dropoff, and all the victims' companions know is that they have somehow disappeared. The only way to move in a white-out is very carefully. It can be the ultimate test of your routefinding skills.

The most frequent white-outs—actually snowstorms—that affect the most people are probably the ones above tree line in the Adirondacks, White Mountains, and Katahdin. The various mountain and hiking clubs there have gone to great effort to mark the trails to help hikers and climbers find their way off high places in these frequent times of limited visibility. Rock cairns several feet high and closely spaced mark many of the trails on the Presidential Range and Franconia Ridge, the two highest and most heavily used ridges in White Mountain National Forest. The people who climb these mountains in winter in "normal" conditions of subzero temperatures and 30-mph wind are just plain tough. There's no place else where people get out of the car when weather conditions are that hostile.

The tempting thing about climbing these relatively low-elevation peaks is that there is not a great distance from tree line to the summits, except for the Presidential Range, where the distance is up to 1800 feet of elevation. Most of these peaks are very accessible, generally being one-day climbs, and the danger of avalanches is mainly in sheltered areas on the lee side. On higher mountains where there is a vast area above timber line, such as the 8000 feet or so of elevation from forest to summit of Mt. Rainier, it is less tempting to tough it out in a storm, and impossible to make a summit climb.

Above Tree Line

This section has been added to the third edition mainly due to the May 1986 accident on Mt. Hood in Oregon. A group of teenagers with adult leaders attempted the summit climb of the 11,245-foot mountain. A storm developed, with high winds, subfreezing temperatures, and blizzard conditions. The decision to turn back was made after some members of the party were too tired and cold to get off the mountain.

A snow cave was dug in which the weaker ones stayed while the two strongest traveled to a road, where help was summoned. The storm continued for several days, which prevented an effective search. By the time the cave was located, only two of the nine who took shelter could be revived.

Many people have run afoul of storms above tree line in spring, summer, and fall in the mountains of the U.S. Site of similar problems in the Washington Cascades is the Goat Rocks, where the Pacific Crest Trail goes over Old Snowy Mountain, an elevation of 7930 feet and well above tree line. One fatality and several near-fatalities have occurred here when a summer-equipped party has encountered winter temperatures and blizzard conditions.

These unpredictable winter-strength storms can be expected from Labor Day (and before) on through autumn and into June the next year. In the eastern mountains, the ferocity and frequency of these storms is of such impact that hiking and climbing clubs and the U.S. Forest Service and other public officials make a great effort to inform the public of the danger. In August 1986, a snowstorm in the Presidential Range led to one death due to hypothermia on Mt. Madison.

Death is a fact in every mountain range in the U.S., as marked by place names like Cadaver Gap on Mt. Rainier and Froze to Death Plateau in the Beartooths of Montana, just two of a long list. Storm-caused fatalities are a significant part of the total mountain death toll.

Like the many drowning victims who never intended to enter the water, a large percentage of people who have died in mountain storms never intended to get into a snowstorm with subfreezing temperatures and severe wind chill. They didn't realize what they had committed themselves to until it was too late to get down the mountain or back out of the storm.

Be aware that encountering storms above tree line exposes you to a far greater risk than does finding yourself in a storm on a forest trail. Include winter clothing in your pack when the trip involves going above tree line. When caught in such a storm, either get the tent up quickly, before your party is too weak and chilled to do so, or turn back while your party has the strength to move into sheltering forest.

Avalanches

By far the most spectacular hazard in winter is the snow avalanche. Large avalanche chutes descending through heavy forest from ridgetop snowfields are easy to recognize and avoid.

Small slides are a greater hazard than huge ones because there are more of them and they aren't as obviously powerful and destructive. Man is totally outmatched when caught in sliding snow: a layer only six inches deep and 20 feet wide sliding less than 100 feet can bury a person.

Big avalanches involve tremendous tonnages of snow and develop a great deal of momentum. Besides ripping out trees on the edge of their paths and in the areas where they stop, they run up opposite slopes. Some travel long distances on level ground after a rapid descent. When speed is high the mass climbs up hillsides where the containing gully makes sharp turns. When the snow drops over a cliff in a gully there is a roar like thunder. Nature on the rampage, as these avalanches testify, is an awesome thing.

There are four main conditions causing snow to slide off mountains. First, during a storm the snow builds up to a depth and weight that exceeds its ability to adhere to the snow or rock surface beneath, so it slides. The majority of avalanches occur during and immediately after storms. Second, wind picks up snow on the windward side of ridges and deposits it on the lee side, or in any sheltered place. This layer may slide during or soon after the storm as a loose, unconsolidated mass. Or it may settle into a firm mass, and over the course of days or weeks the bond between it and the surface below may weaken until the entire layer slides as a slab. It is not necessary for snow to drift anywhere to form slab. The fact that snow falls when the wind is blowing is sufficient to cause it to form a wind slab that may slide soon after the snow is deposited or remain unstable days or weeks later. The third condition is a rising temperature that melts the newly fallen snow. The mass is lubricated by this moisture, and the bond with the underlying snow is decreased until either the upper layer or the whole mass slides. The fourth is depth hoar. The formation of these frost crystals at depth in the snowpack weakens the bond between two layers of snow.

The study of avalanches is complex and technical. Experts spend their winters collecting data on snowfall, temperatures, and wind velocity and dig countless pits to observe layers and measure densities with penetrometers. They are gaining much information on why snow slides in avalanches.

Unfortunately the casual snow traveler may overlook or ignore the data and interpretation of avalanche hazard. Certain areas that are heavily used for winter recreation and main highways that are constantly subject to avalanches do have day-to-day avalanche warnings posted. The U.S. Forest Service has expanded its avalanche warning system in the last few years. Ski areas patrol and check danger areas daily.

There is a great deal of up-to-date information available on the mountain snow slide hazard; snowshoers should take advantage of it. Radio and TV ski reports give a general picture of local or regional snow conditions so it's best to do some specific research before setting out on a hike or climb in avalanche-prone country. However, most of us who love the solitude of the remote winter backcountry are pretty much on our own.

At times winter hikers attempt a field study to understand more about avalanches. I've helped dig a lot of holes and snow caves in Cascade snow but never found out anything about depth hoar, for example: the subzero temperatures necessary to create depth hoar are not common in this relatively warm area. So it is probably of more value to an individual to learn to recognize where avalanches occur than to understand exactly why the snow cuts loose and swoops down mountainsides.

The great treeless slashes through forest and the vast expanses of steep open slopes on western mountains and steep lee slopes above the tree line of the Presidentials and Katahdin in the East are obvious spots where avalanches occur. This chapter will give enough pointers that a perceptive beginner can go out in such mountain country with no undue fears about avalanches. Anyone can recognize the danger in big avalanche slopes and gullies. The hard part is to take action on what you know when in the gray area of a possible hazard on a small, moderately steep, open slope.

One important factor that has a bearing on avalanches, usually of the slab type, is known as depth hoar. This is a zone or layer of distinctive cup- or needle-shaped crystals, caused by water vapor either from the ground or from the lower layers of the snowpack rising and refreezing within the snowpack. Vapor rises through the snowpack all winter long. It may freeze on the surface at about 0°F and look like frost "feathers"; this is called surface hoar.

If the temperature drops well below zero the upper part of the snowpack is chilled to air temperature and water vapor freezes at some depth rather than on the surface—thus the term depth hoar. These crystals do not bond together and therefore form a weak layer within the snowpack which acts like an air space. On steep slopes anything that breaks the overlying layer of snow causes a slide as the depth hoar layer helps weaken or destroy the bond with the snow below. There is a "whoomp" as the upper layers collapse and settle.

Depth hoar is most likely to form in any weak layers or crust within the snowpack. These have been noted under ice layers in the east. Because water vapor cannot rise through this barrier, depth hoar forms, which snowshoers discover as the upper layers settle. The longer the severe subzero temperature persists, the deeper the snowpack is chilled, so depth hoar may form right on the ground. For example, one February a group of us started on a climbing trip in the Purcell Range in British Columbia. Several weeks of –20° to –30°F temperatures had created a depth hoar layer through the Rockies and other ranges in Canada.

Pits we dug in the four-foot-deep snowpack showed that the bottom 15 to 18 inches was depth hoar. A snow cave in a nine-foot-deep drift at 7200 feet showed the same. Mountaineering was out of the question, so we substituted a route protected by dense forest to Lake of the Hanging Glacier. Everywhere we went the slab settled under us.

Cracks radiated out from us on the level logging road approach. Cracks appeared under the trail-breaker's snowshoes, and every 50 yards or so the "whoomp" of settling slab jarred our nerves. Cracks appeared on the edges of the trail and around trees, and small bushes shook, but after several days the sound almost lost its shock value as we nearly became accustomed to it. During our stay more and more slab avalanche fracture lines appeared on slopes of the 10,000- and 11,000-foot peaks high above our forest-protected route. The most valuable information we received on avoiding trouble was from our guide, Arnör Larson, who has climbed for years in winter in the Purcells and is knowledgeable about avalanche hazards there.

Depth hoar is not supposed to be a hazard on glaciers. It is doubtful that water vapor would rise hundreds of feet through glacial ice and refreeze as hoar beneath the surface snowpack. However, at the time of our outing, over the previous two months 10 skiers had lost their lives in depth hoar-associated slab avalanches in British Columbia alone. Our party decided to stay off steep glaciers that looked like superb avalanche terrain and let someone else field test the validity of whether there is depth hoar on glaciers.

When a layer of snow is unstable, anything that disturbs it can trigger a slide—a snowshoer, a skier, snow falling out of a tree or from a cliff above. Avalanche control methods in ski areas and on highways include explosives to trigger the snow into sliding or to stabilize it further when it will not slide.

Avalanches follow gullies off the sides of ridges and down mountain faces. These may be spotted easily where there is forest cover. Lee slopes below cornices are common areas of wind slab. Snow cornices indicate lots of windblown snow on the side they overhang. Forest cover isn't foolproof, as snow can slide through fairly closely spaced trees like water, inflicting additional injuries as the victim ricochets off trees. Only if the trees are "as thick as the hair on a dog's back," to quote one U.S. Forest Service ranger, can you be sure it will not slide. In one actual instance, a slide filtered a skier through very closely set trees, stripping him of skis, poles, hat, glasses, and mitts and inflicting severe injuries.

Powder snow avalanches generally occur at high elevations where temperatures remain cold. Much powder snow sloughs off the steepest slopes during storms; it is most dangerous where wind has deposited piles of it in sheltered gullies. The speed of the sliding snow is great, and the air pushed ahead of the avalanche results in a preceding wind blast that is as destructive as the snow itself. The powder snow menace is not usually as severe on the volcanic peaks of the Cascades, possibly because they are quite rounded and have few high sheltering ridges where it can collect. On these open slopes the wind packs the snow as it falls. However, there are places on Mt. Rainier where windblown snow accumulates and creates avalanche danger. Between 11,000 and 12,000 feet the Ingraham Glacier, in the lee of Gibraltar Rock, catches enough snow to plug, or at least cover, its many huge crevasses each winter. At another point just under 7000 feet, Panorama Point faces into the prevailing southwest wind. Here it forms both slab and powder avalanches that have killed a few of the many people who have snowshoed, skied, and hiked up it toward 10,000-foot Camp Muir.

When a pile of windblown snow on a lee slope congeals into a somewhat solid mass, it is called a slab. As it settles, the slab adheres to itself and tends to shrink, and the process weakens the bond with the underlying layer. The joint between the two layers may develop depth hoar during a spell of –20°F or so temperatures. This zone is less dense than either the slab above or the slab below, and the area sounds hollow underfoot. As the bond weakens, it eventually reaches a point at which the slightest jar can trigger a slide. When it slides, the slab, several inches to several feet in depth, breaks off from stable snow in a vertical fracture that may run for several hundred feet. The sliding mass may start over a large area and break into many blocks. The danger in a slab avalanche is that many tons of snow may remain poised for weeks and then be released all at once. Apparently not as sensitive to rising temperature as powder snow, many slabs are triggered in the Cascades in April and May when overhanging cornices crash onto the snow below. Of course cornices themselves, which may form on both sides of a ridge within a short distance, are a hazard to anyone below, whether they trigger any further avalanche or not.

Slab is formed by conditions of heavy snowfall and high winds in mountains and hills, and even on flats. These slabs on flat areas also sound hollow and sometimes settle a little with a "whoomp." If the snow on the flats is settling as you snowshoe over it, there will be slab formations on the ridges too. And if the road cuts have slab avalanches spontaneously released on them, the high country is no place to be. Normally the deeper your web sinks, the firmer the snow becomes, but occasionally your snowshoe settles through the snow, which seems to be hollow, or softer, underneath. This may be an indication that you should not venture out on steep, high mountain slopes for a few days until the snow has stabilized.

The only sure way to check for slab avalanche hazard is to dig a pit and make a simple test (Figure 26). This involves carrying a shovel, which should be a requirement for outings in avalanche terrain anyway. Choice of a spot to dig requires some thought. It should be in a spot that will not avalanche, but the pit should be in snow of the same structure as the slope that is of concern.

Probably at the side of the slope, but within the forest or some other protection, is the safest spot. Dig the pit all the way to the ground to check it out thoroughly. Areas with slab avalanche hazard don't usually have 10–15 feet of snow, so the job is not as formidable as it sounds.

Leave a protruding section on the uphill side of the pit, as in Figure 26. Cut the wall down smooth and run a finger down it

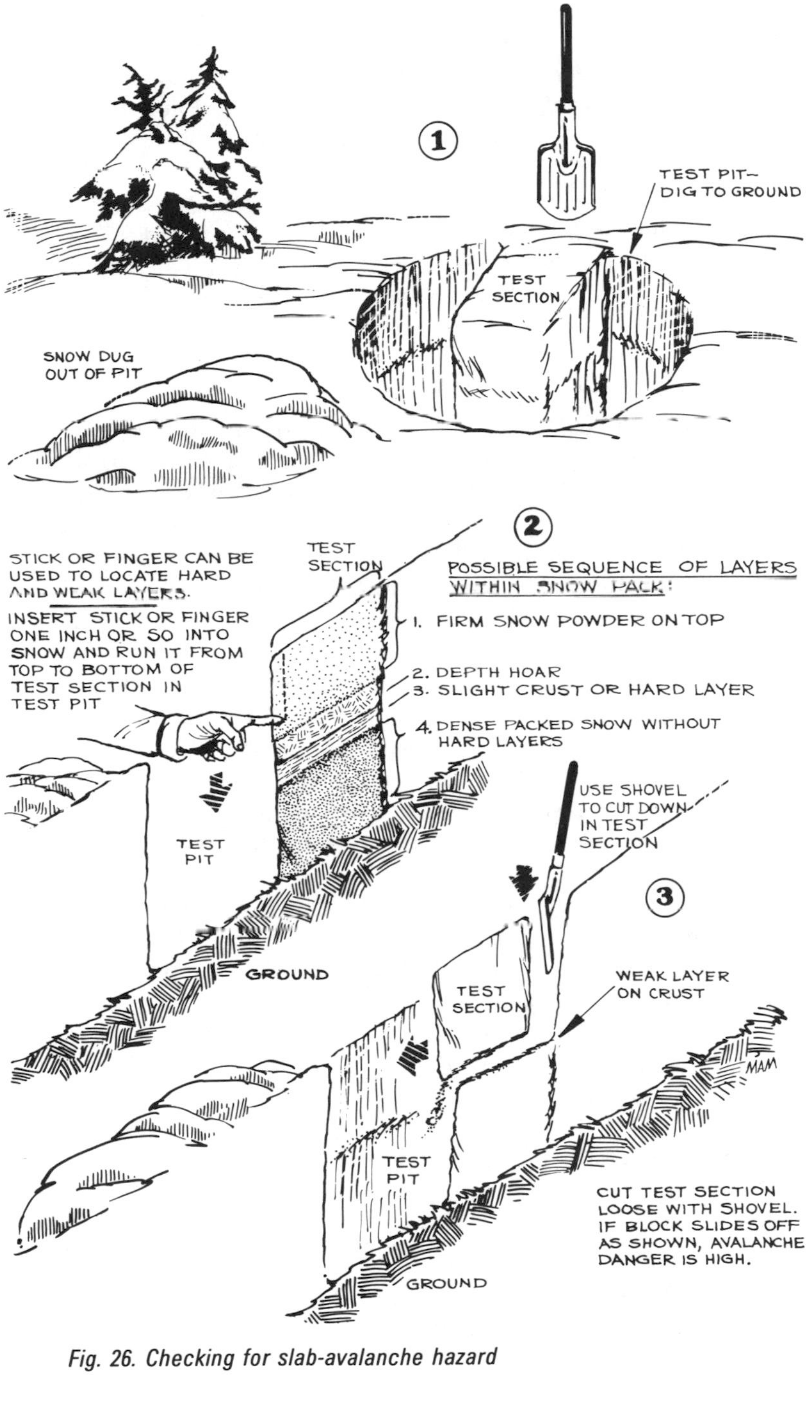

Fig. 26. Checking for slab-avalanche hazard

to note hard layers. Check visually for snow crystals that indicate depth hoar. Needle- and cup-shaped crystals do not consolidate and thus indicate a hazard. Use a dark-colored mitten for background and a small magnifying glass to check thoroughly.

The final check is with the shovel. Cut down through the snow on the protruding section of wall, as illustrated. If the layers of snow slide off, there is danger of an avalanche, so don't proceed out on the slope with this hazardous snow on it.

Different mountain regions of the country have different avalanche hazards that depend on weather conditions. A brief survey is in order.

Pacific Northwest: Wet snow avalanches are the most predictable type and are most typical of the wet, warm Pacific Northwest. The textbook sequence of events leading to release of these heavy, relatively slow-moving slides is as follows: cold, moist air from the Pacific Ocean moves across the Cascades, dropping several feet of snow. This air mass is pushed out by a warmer one; the snow is warmed to melting, becomes wet, and settles. Weight increases as it picks up water from the warm, moist air. The bond between the new snow and the underlying layer becomes lubricated and the mass slides. Wet snow a few inches to several feet in depth can slide. Weight is very great although speed is slow when compared to powder snow. Wet snow rolls into balls, ranging from a few inches in size to several feet across. It normally freezes to ice when it stops.

There are also powder snow and wind slab avalanches in the Cascades. Winter avalanche hazard may begin as early as October and does not end until May, June, or July, depending on late-season storms.

Eastern Mountains: Here the greatest hazard from avalanches occurs on the lee sides of the Presidential Range and Mt. Katahdin; they usually are the wind slab variety. Depth hoar can be a factor as temperatures frequently drop well below zero. There is also the possibility of ice layers from January thaws, which have an effect on depth hoar formation as well as forming a good base for avalanches.

The areas of greatest hazard are the exposed lee slopes above tree line, and the slides, treeless chutes descending from mountaintops to forest.

Tuckerman and Huntington Ravine headwalls are heavily

climbed and skied once they are snowcovered. These steep glacial cirques avalanche often after each snowfall, and avalanche warnings are posted daily at Pinkham Notch. The most recent fatality was a rescue team member on the Lions Head Trail in 1984. Avalanches also endanger the steep headwalls and slides in less traveled Great Gulf, King Ravine and above tree line on Franconia Ridge and Katahdin, to mention only a few.

Wet snow slides occur as temperatures warm in spring; these are not as much snowshoeing hazards as they are spring mountaineering dangers.

Rockies: It's hard to generalize about an area as large as the Rockies and associated ranges of Wyoming, Montana, Colorado, New Mexico, Arizona, Idaho, British Columbia, and Alberta. Normally the subzero cold of December and January causes depth hoar formation. Subsequent snowfalls insulate it, and it may persist into February and March or later. The result is a serious avalanche hazard on slopes; later snowfall with wind and resultant wind slab, and slab formed from snowfall without wind, may increase the hazard.

Only by checking in the field can the degree of danger be determined. Snow may firm by March to make good traveling. Snowshoers in the Colorado Rockies feel there is a greater slab-avalanche hazard in Wyoming than in Colorado. Warm days in late winter and spring consolidate the snow and depth hoar, but on north slopes the hazard persists longer. The local climbers get avalanched frequently enough to give ample warning about the danger that depth hoar and wind slab create. It is sensible to use information from every agency and authority when planning a mountain trip in these areas. Fortunately, there are untouched areas for touring and hiking that are not menaced by slides. Every winter Yellowstone National Park plays host to more people on touring skis.

Colorado and the mountains to the north have some similar avalanche hazards. Subzero temperatures form depth hoar, which creates severe hazard. Subsequent snowfall, as in all other depth hoar areas, insulates the hoar zone deep within the snowpack, preserving it until warmer late winter or spring temperatures consolidate it.

Sometimes by February deep, soft snow has firmed up and traveling is easier. Snow above timber line may be stable earlier, as wind and sun firm it sooner than on shaded slopes and under trees in the forested areas. By early April there is often lots of sun, which may warm the snowpack to form a crust on which snowshoers can bare-boot it. In comparison to the Cascades, there is lots of sun all winter long.

Some years, March and April see heavy snowfall with wind and resultant wind slab. Again, avalanche warnings for highways and ski areas give valuable information to the snow traveler. People not familiar with the area should use all facilities, such as these and U.S. Forest Service snow and avalanche reports, as well as locating a local authority or knowledgeable person before starting out on a mountain trip. Generalizations are helpful, but only a field check on snow formation in the area you intend to use will provide valid avalanche hazard information.

When avalanche hazard is high, pick hikes and climbs free of danger. These will be in the lower, gentler hills, which are a part of the extensive and complex ranges of Colorado. The U.S. Forest Service Avalanche Center at Fort Collins, Colorado, provides up-to-date avalanche forecasts. It is at the Rocky Mountain Forest and Range Experiment Station.

Wasatch: The same general weather pattern as the Rockies occurs in the Wasatch of Utah. Deep powder snow is to be expected in December and January with spells of severe subzero temperatures that cause the formation of depth hoar. Snow usually falls with the wind, causing wind slab, especially in the high mountains. Movies at the U.S. Forest Service Avalanche Study Center near Alta, Utah, testify to the danger of slab avalanches, whether influenced by wind slab or depth hoar.

Deep snow over the depth hoar layer may cause it to persist throughout the winter, as in other mountain areas described already. South slopes firm up earliest, but south slopes warmed by the sun in later winter present the greatest spring avalanche hazard, generally of the wet snow type.

Winter may begin in October, and powder snow can still be expected at higher elevations through April and May. Heavy storms may occur any month, as the storm patterns within each area are capricious. Once more, use all avalanche warning information that is available. There are avalanche-free routes on gentler terrain and smaller peaks north of the main Wasatch.

Sierra: These mountains also have severe early winter subzero weather with its resultant depth hoar formation. The depth hoar layer often lasts through the winter as subsequent snowfalls cover it, insulating the weak zone from warmth that tends to stabilize the snowpack. Normal snowfall is several feet deep, although there are drought years when snowfall is light. Winter can begin in late September and October, but late November and December is more usual. Deep powder with danger of wind slab is usual in December, January, and February. The weather pattern in this vast mountain area is as changeable as each of the other winter areas discussed. March, April, and even May can be months of greatest snowfall.

Spring slab avalanches can be due to depth hoar formed in early winter. Often by February snow is firm enough for good snow travel in the foothills east of the main Sierra and the southern California peaks. By March and April the snow on the high peaks and valleys may firm up. This depends entirely on the weather pattern for the year, and avalanche danger and travel conditions must be evaluated on the spot. Ski area and highway avalanche warnings are a real help, as in the other areas where people snowshoe and tour.

There is much discussion among snowshoers of what to do when caught in an avalanche. If you can still think and react to the situation it seems best to get on your back, trying to stay on top of the sliding snow with swimming motions of the legs and arms, and attempt to work to one side. Try to use your arms to keep a breathing space in front of your face. If you are standing and the snow you are on begins to slide, sit facing downhill.

Regard your efforts as a fight for your life and do everything possible to achieve that end. If your hand, foot, or clothing or attached equipment is visible on the surface, your companions are very likely to recover you alive. Your evasive action may keep you from getting buried, or you may crawl out of a partial burial on your own. A victim found in less than 15 minutes, especially if buried less than one foot deep, will have an 80 percent chance of surviving. At 30 minutes and two feet deep, the chances are less than 50 percent for survival. The longer the time and deeper the burial, the grimmer the survival statistics.

Remember that after the finding there will probably be some digging, and avalanche snow is often very dense and packed hard when the slide stops. Have more than one shovel in your party in case the one shovel is buried with the victim.

The best cure is prevention: minimize the time you are exposed to the danger. Cross narrow chutes one person at a time with lookouts posted to warn of an approaching slide. If the day is becoming very warm and there is deep new snow with no recent avalanches around, get to a protected place. Wet snow slides are more frequent on warm afternoons than on crisp cold mornings. If there is no way around an avalanche hazard, the outing must be ended. Some persons who are exposed to avalanches use avalanche cord, dark-colored nylon cord about an eighth of an inch in diameter and up to 100 feet long. One end is tied to the waist and the rest is dragged when crossing a particularly dangerous area. Should a person be caught in a slide, there is a good chance that part of the cord will show, telling rescuers where to start digging.

Experience in mountaineering and skiing increase your chances of getting caught in an avalanche. A limited study showed 69 avalanche fatalities were people with advanced skills, 13 were intermediates, and 11 were novices. Chances are it took highly skilled people to get far enough from the car in winter to enter avalanche country. The beginners just weren't tough enough to get to where they could get killed!

Restraint in avoiding high avalanche hazard comes hard to the male of the species. A study of avalanche deaths in the U.S. from 1950–1987 by Betsy R. Armstrong of Fulcrum, Inc., Golden, Colorado, showed that 88 percent of these deaths were men, the highest concentration being in the 20–29 age group. It would appear that to try to warn people—especially males—of the possibility of getting killed enjoying winter recreation in a beautiful mountain setting is about as effective as warning people about AIDS; a minority by their actions deny that anything that much fun in such an attractive setting could have a hidden hazard.

Actually, no one seems to have very satisfactory evasive tactics or secrets of survival. My own experience in two avalanches was that it was over so quickly there wasn't time to do very much. Both times I turned and faced downhill. In a few seconds my feet worked through the sliding snow and caught in the layer underneath, then the sliding snow behind pitched me forward on hands and knees. This is not the way to ride an avalanche because my head could have hit any obstruction first and the powder eddying around my face made breathing difficult. Once at the mercy of the avalanche I no longer had any choice in matters of direction and position.

Avalanche victim detectors—small radio transceivers that transmit a radio signal that can be received by a similar unit—

are available. The unit on a buried victim transmits a signal, speeding location of the person—provided there is another unit on a person not buried.

For the detector to be of value, all members of a party must have one and they must wear it, not store it in a pack, which can be swept away in an avalanche. During regular activities, the transceiver's three-way switch (transmit-receive-off) must be set to transmit.

Tracking the detector's signal takes some practice. Try locating a buried transceiver. With your detector set to receive and ear piece firmly set in your ear, walk around so you pick up the signal or beep. The closer you are, the louder the beep. Mark the place, and continue beyond to determine that the signal gets weaker. Sometimes there will be a second place with a strong signal, but this is something like a "skip" in short-wave radio and is actually some yards from the buried instrument.

Return to the marked place, and move away in several directions to get the best location. The area of strongest signal isn't always pinpointed to a square-foot area but may be a circle 8 to 10 feet across. Practice will increase your skill so you don't have to dig a room-sized area.

In areas of managed avalanche control, a snowshoer can run an additional risk. Explosive artillery shells are fired at ridges above roads and human habitation to trigger small slides before the snow becomes deep enough to cause a really damaging avalanche. Be sure to check with local authorities before entering areas subject to such control.

There is no accurate way of predicting the hour, day, or week of most slides. The longer the exposure to danger the greater the likelihood of getting caught. The best you can do is to recognize that deep, unconsolidated snow on open slopes and gullies is likely to slide soon after a storm. Be wary of fairly gentle slopes of 20 degrees or so; these may lure people onto them because they don't look as hazardous as 45 degrees or steeper. Warming weather after a heavy snowfall will quickly cause avalanches. Lee slopes are very likely to avalanche after heavy snowfall accompanied by high winds, and the danger remains for weeks after the storm.

Obviously the only 100-percent sure way to avoid getting caught in an avalanche is not to be in a place where there might be one. There is seldom any totally safe time in the mountains during winter and into early spring. The higher elevations do not firm up as soon as lower slopes. Cornices fall off ridgetops until June or later.

The conditions I prefer for a trip in the Cascades into an area of avalanche hazard are several days of warm, clear weather following a storm, then clear, cold, stable weather. The warm weather should flush off the avalanches and cold temperatures stabilize the snow.

Each range has its weather pattern. Experienced judgment is the only way to assess the danger, and then it must be based on knowledge of recent weather and the terrain. Use all available information that has a bearing on avalanches. Weather and snowfall reports and temperature patterns can tell you a great deal about what is happening in the mountains. Mountain pass highway reports are valuable, plus avalanche warnings at ski areas and many U.S. national forests. The only choice you have, in the final analysis, is to turn back and not put yourself in an area of potential danger, or continue and accept the risk. But spending the remainder of your life in the few seconds it takes an avalanche to run really doesn't seem to be a truly meaningful snowshoe experience.

Three books are excellent resources for further study: *International Handbook of Mountain Rescue* by Hamish MacInnes, *ABC of Avalanche Safety* by E.R. La Chapelle, and *Avalanches and Snow Safety* by Colin Fraser. Avalanche lectures are a part of most winter outing programs sponsored by hiking and climbing clubs. There are also avalanche schools in most mountain areas. Rather than list all, I'll include here two of the better known:

National Avalanche School
National Ski Patrol Systems
133 S. Van Gordon St., Suite 100
Lakewood, CO 80228

American Avalanche Institute
Box 308
Wilson, WY 83014

Search and Rescue

Over the years people have become lost, been injured, or been killed in the mountains and backcountry through avalanches, hypothermia, and other hazards, so a chain of responsibility has developed to organize and put into action search and search and rescue procedures. In Washington, the county sheriffs have been delegated this authority, although certain areas, such as national parks and Indian reservations, have their own organizations independent of state or local control. In New Hampshire, the Department of Fish and Game has this job, and in the national parks of Canada the park wardens are in charge. Although there is no real pattern in the various states, provinces, counties, or towns, rescue responsibility has generally been delegated to an agency or person wherever there is outdoor recreation.

The range of problems connected with winter rescues is interesting. The mountain areas of New England are quite compact compared with the many western ranges. The British Columbia director of emergencies has a vast expanse of mountain country and also must be concerned with hunters lost somewhere along logging roads 1000 miles (1600 km) long.

As agency personnel changes, so does expertise at rescue. There are exceptions, but few sheriffs or game protectors have experienced people with specialized skills on their staff, so in many areas good working arrangements with winter climbers fill this need. Thus much search and rescue work is done by local volunteers under the umbrella of the responsible agency. Most of the burden of evacuation is now borne by helicopters, but there is enough bad weather that grounds aircraft to guarantee that foot-propelled people are still a vital part of the rescue picture. Search dogs trained to locate victims buried in avalanches are in great demand for these emergencies. Well-trained dogs and their owners are flown thousands of miles to smell out victims buried in flood debris as well as in snow.

There is no uniform method of determining how backcountry emergencies should be handled. The traditional method of obtaining help is to get word to the local sheriff (or to a ranger if in a national park). In Washington, for example, the sheriff then evaluates the problem and starts organizing the search or rescue. This may involve getting medical aid, calling for volunteers—usually Search and Rescue and Mountain Rescue units—to bring the person out, arranging for a helicopter, setting up an air search, bringing in a canine search group, or a combination of methods. State Civil Defense usually helps coordinate efforts, especially if several state and federal agencies are contributing to the operation. Jeep clubs or Explorer Scout Search and Rescue groups may participate. For large searches, several branches may be involved, using Air Force, Army, and Navy helicopters as well as Civil Air Patrol.

The helicopter has become the real backbone of the backcountry rescue, but the availability of helicopters from MAST—Military Aid for Safety and Traffic—may vary, depending on military involvement elsewhere. Occasionally Coast Guard choppers are also available. Performance has been improved so much since the 1950s that injured climbers have been lifted off Mt. McKinley at over 17,000 feet and Mountain Rescue people have been flown to 14,000 feet on Mt. Rainier, then picked up again.

Winter snow closes many access roads and complicates search and rescue. Bad weather is likely to be a factor, too, hampering the use of helicopters and light planes. In fact, just about every wheel- and foot-propelled search group can be stalled on the steps of the sheriff's office. Deep snow isolates the backcountry: a 10-mile round trip in rough country in average snow conditions can be considered a strenuous day on snowshoes. A rescue party on foot needs to carry overnight gear and set up an advance base camp just to get to the backcountry; instead of a quick dash up a trail to the location of the problem, the winter rescue lasts several days to accomplish anything. Obviously people on foot are frequently not able to get to the victim soon enough. Snowmobiles have a good potential for increasing the range of a search party, but the machines move too fast for thorough search and are limited almost entirely to roads in mountain country. Food-powered rescuers may have an aversion to snow machines and few snowmobilers have any experience in searching, let alone snowshoeing. A combination of methods is usually the solution.

For example, in one incident jeeps and snowmobiles were used to transport Tacoma Mountain Rescue People and a German Shepherd Search Group to Corral Pass, north of Mt. Rainier, to search for a hunter who had been missing overnight. By getting to the search area quickly and easily, the foot searchers were able to search strenuously and effectively. The hunter was located, and although he was disoriented and somewhat incoherent, he walked out under his own power after being warmed with hot drinks.

Later the same year a similar situation occurred in the east central Washington Cascades. Another hunter was missing in temperatures of about 10°F. The sheriff called in Ellensburg Mountain Rescue and Snowmobile Search and Rescue personnel and a search was begun about 11:00 P.M. on snowmobiles. They were successful in locating the missing man's trail, although it entered country too rugged to follow on machines. It was clear that the victim must be followed on foot, and two men did so while snowmobiles patrolled roads on the edges of the area. The search was completed when the hunter walked out the next afternoon, with the foot searchers only about half an hour behind him.

As more and more people go out in the hills for winter recreation, it is logical to assume that from time to time they will find themselves in need of outside help. Summer rescue techniques work in winter except for the added problem of snow-covered access roads, which make it difficult to rapidly get to the area where the problem is.

Aircraft are another object of winter searches. Unfortunately their range is so great that only other aircraft can search for them effectively. Planes are usually the victims of bad weather and this in turn prevents any immediate air search, so at times authorities solicit foot-powered volunteers to search an area in the faint hope that they will stumble onto the wreckage.

Washington Mountain Rescue winter training conferences have established that no single rescue organization is adequate to handle a problem 5 to 10 miles from a road in winter. Rescuers on snowshoes and skis are too limited in range to move quickly enough. If they must carry overnight equipment and food for several days, their speed and range are further curtailed. Add to this the general lack of enthusiasm of trained rescue personnel for winter outings and the result is a greatly reduced number of people available for such problems. Winter training programs, spending at least one night in a snow camp, have not been overattended. (Personnel for one program received inquiries about the accommodations at the motel convention center nearby.) Winter demands a great deal of searchers, which only experience or training sessions in winter can provide.

People who frequent the winter backcountry need to be the basis for improving present backcountry rescue groups. It is good insurance to be an active participant in a functioning group that can get out and help people in trouble in the winter hills. I've limped out after being somewhat mistreated by sliding snow, and a number of other people have had even narrower escapes than that. There is no better motivation than knowing the rescue group you are helping to train may someday come and get you out of trouble.

Again, preparation is invaluable. In case of accident in your own party in the backcountry, what are you going to do if you need outside help? First, of course, objectively evaluate the situation—don't waste time analyzing the cause. If the problem is an injury, care for the victim and get help. Consider shorter routes out to a road, if any exist. If you need help quickly and there is a good shortcut to a road, go, and later figure out how to get back to your car.

There is a public awareness of more people frequenting the winter hills. Fortunately there is also an organized volunteer group of rescue people near most of the winter hiking and climbing areas, whether it's backwoods Canada, New England, or the West. Increased publicity does help to encourage talented winter hikers and climbers to offer their services. Unfortunately, the emphasis sometimes is that a death or injury to a winter hiker is a tragedy and someone should put a stop to this sort of nonsense. My personal philosophy on backcountry accidents is that death and injury are a part of life and occur at home, too, which is supposedly a safer place to be.

Do give some thought and time to the subject of winter rescue. If you are asked to participate in such an operation, consider it an honor. Sometimes, in our impersonal and affluent society, one has the impression that no one needs a helping hand. But if someone is in trouble in the mountains in winter, that person needs help, and may need it desperately.

CHAPTER 11

Illness and Injury

Unlike the special safety hazards of winter, the problems discussed in this chapter are, except in unusual circumstances, preventable. Proper equipment, good judgment, and careful attention to early warning signs should make their occurrence as unlikely as some rare tropical disease, but there is always a crop of neophytes, or an old-timer who has not learned his lessons well. Any small problem such as a minor injury is intensified by winter conditions; cold is the catalyst that can create real trouble from difficulties that might be joked about in summer.

In a typical situation, a party is caught by a storm in a remote area. The first reaction is to continue. Someone becomes tired, so others lend a hand, and they all keep going. Soon it becomes apparent that they cannot make it out, so they decide to stay overnight. By this time everyone is too wet or cold and tired to set up good shelter, and because they never intended to camp in a storm, they did not bring the necessary equipment to do so. This can and does happen in summer, but it is obviously more serious in winter.

The combination of fatigue, wet clothing, and cold weather puts too great a strain on an individual with a physical weakness. An undiagnosed minor heart problem or infection in this situation can be fatal. Some people who have become severely chilled may simply die, although others equally miserable survive.

In actual cases in which these conditions have occurred, and in which there have been fatalities, the party has tried to take care of its own problems—the first step in any emergency. But safety is due more to advance preparation than to individual or group heroics during an emergency. If the groups that experienced the fatalities had carried adequate overnight gear the outcome might have been very different.

A lightweight two-person tent can provide very good bivouac protection. Four people can crowd into it and, seated on foam pads, arrange themselves fairly comfortably. Probably the best way is to sit with two people in one end, facing the other two in the opposite end. This can be done without tent poles or pegs, providing you aren't on a steep snow slope, where a platform would need to be dug. The main problems are that excessive moisture from breath requires ventilation and a resultant heat loss, and that the part of one's body that is tightly pressed against the tent will be cold. Packs or extra clothes might insulate these spots.

A small, lightweight tent thus will shelter four people where a sleeping bag, foam pad, and tarp leave the two or three who can't get in the sleeping bag poorly sheltered. The advantages of sitting facing each other in pairs—or whatever number of people are in the party—is that feet and legs can be overlapped for more comfort than four seated crosswise. Second, cold or frosted toes can be treated easily, and people's faces can be watched to check on each other's well-being. A glassy stare might indicate a need for warming. Conversation is easier when facing a person, and some cheering up is sometimes most desirable during the endless hours of a forced winter bivouac.

Hypothermia

Hypothermia is a more precise name for what is still often referred to as exposure. The problem is that the victim is unable to maintain normal body temperature. When inner body temperature drops below 98.6°F, shivering begins and coordination becomes poor. If chilling continues until body temperature is about 88°F, shivering stops and the victim becomes disoriented and enters a stupor. Unless something is done to stop the loss of body heat and restore normal body temperature, the victim will lose consciousness and die. The air temperature may not be below +50°F, and the victim may have no frostbite or frozen fingertips or toes.

A person who is dehydrated is more subject to chilling and hypothermia than one who is well hydrated. It takes about two quarts of fluid a day to maintain a good fluid balance in your body. Drink enough water so you urinate several times a day. If it stains the snow a deep orange, better drink more water. The concentrated color indicates a lack of water in your system. You lose a surprising amount of water when breathing cold air, not to mention sweating when snowshoeing hard with too many clothes on.

Diagnosis of hypothermia is simple; the person is thoroughly chilled, probably very tired, somewhat disoriented, and has poor coordination. Someone who can be warmed will soon be back to normal, but if hypothermia occurs when a party is lost in a snowstorm and has no tent or tarps, the problem is serious. If a tent is available, set it up, strip off wet clothing, and place the victim in a sleeping bag with another person in good condition who can provide body-to-body warmth; or fill canteens with warm—not hot—water and put them in the bag. Hot drinks may suffice if the condition is not serious.

Treatment for hypothermia should be preventive. Be alert to early symptoms and warm chilled people before they become disoriented or enter the advanced stages. The serious hypothermia case develops when there is no easy way to provide shelter. Adequate shelter, hard work, and some real adapting to miserable weather are necessary to warm a badly chilled person in a winter storm or to bring a person already hypothermic at nightfall through the night alive.

It is surprising that a badly hypothermic person, often semiconscious or unconscious, will die in the course of being rescued and warmed. This has mystified rescue personnel.

The explanation was confirmed during post mortem examinations of hypothermia victims, including analysis of their blood. Two factors in particular caused the heart stoppage, and other factors were contributors to the death. Warming the victim started blood circulation from the extremities. This blood was still below 98.6°F and very acidic due to the accumulation of impurities while it was not circulating. The heart, which was already under considerable stress, quit functioning at the added shock of receiving cold, acidic blood.

Understanding of this danger has led to a change in the treatment of severely hypothermic people. The unconscious or semiconscious hypothermia victim should not be warmed in the field but should be transported to a hospital medical facility, which can control warming and prevent the shock to the heart of cold, acidic blood. The responsibility of the rescue party is to evacuate the unconscious as gently as possible. Jarring or bumping the victim may also contribute to heart stoppage.

Tents, sleeping bags, and foam pads provide the best shelter and insulation, but even these must be properly used and only expedition-quality tents can survive winter storms above tree line; otherwise camp must be made in some sheltered place.

Nylon tarps may provide some protection in a sheltered area, but insulation is required underneath for sitting on the snow. Plastic tarps won't survive in a wind, but they can be used as a ground cloth, or several people can wrap up in one and huddle together for warmth.

Snow caves are excellent protection, but it takes about two hours to dig a minimal cave for two with a shovel, and even then you must have insulation. With a stove in the party, and thus heat to dry the gear and prepare hot fluid to warm chilled bodies, a snow cave becomes quite livable.

A snow trench or shelter built among living, uncut boughs under a tree are other alternatives, both requiring shovel and tarps to provide any degree of protection in winter. Wind and snow blow through the boughs, but they may help break the wind if you can wrap up in a tarp. A trench will quickly drift full unless there is a good tarp for a roof.

An igloo is excellent shelter but requires more skill to construct than a snow cave. It is also time-consuming and requires a snow saw, perhaps a shovel, and again a foam pad. (For more on snow shelters, see chapter 12.) Good physical condition is an invaluable deterrent to the "psyching out" that can affect you if you are tired, cold, and lost. Choose companions who are in good condition and choose objectives within your capabilities. To screen out persons who fatigue easily and to work yourself into excellent shape, take short hikes before trying a long, arduous one. If you are with a bunch of tigers it may be possible to persevere through the worst of conditions; if anything goes wrong you are much better off than with a soft group whose members are new at the activity.

Plan what to do if you are running late, get lost, or become confused. Assume leadership and force a stop to set up camp before the party is exhausted, cold, and about to collapse. Avoid leading a weak group on a tough trip. It's fine to be the strongest in the party until it becomes a life or death matter, but a close call from an avalanche or storm or a fatality due to your own poor judgment is not easy to live with in the years ahead. Most of all, learn when to turn back.

Check the weather. Storm clouds are dismal everywhere. In fact, it's worse in a storm on the inspiring peaks than in the foothill forests. For the high mountains, wait for good weather; you will make miles with less effort and have a view beyond description.

If the temperature is zero degrees or colder, be especially careful not to overextend yourself or the group. If you are in cold country where zero is normal, then be extremely careful when the temperature drops to –30°F. Be ready to return to the car if someone is too tired or feet or fingers become too cold.

Frostbite

If you are planning a winter trip to a colder range, be prepared for a real shock. For example, if your home area is the "warm" Cascades, then experiencing live the bitter cold wind of the eastern mountains is memorable. As much as possible make adequate psychological as well as physical preparation for the blow. Many snowshoe climbs are called off when it gets down to 0°F in the Cascades. It's quite interesting to watch New England climbers on Willy's Slide at Crawford Notch, New Hampshire, when the temperature is zero and a 10-mph breeze is blowing. The natives will be sitting around comfortably eating lunch without wrapping up in a down jacket. The body I wear has difficulty trying to prepare for zero weather by sitting around at Snoqualmie Pass, Washington, where mixed rain and snow are falling and the temperature is +31.9°F.

It is less painful to adapt to above-freezing weather when you're used to icy temperatures—although even when sweat is running down their faces, people who by long habit wear wool fishnet tops, wool shirt, wool cap, and windbreaker have trouble stripping down for Pacific Coast conditions. Habit makes it difficult to unhook heavy mitts and cord from around their necks, take the water bottle out of their shirts, and stuff both in the pack. Sometimes someone has to tell them to get the windbreaker off and unbutton the wool shirt for ventilation before heat exhaustion becomes a problem.

During extremely cold weather a person may freeze the tip of the nose, cheek, ear, finger, or toe during an outing, but unless an entire foot or hand is frozen, this is not too serious. Flesh is damaged first by freezing and then may die of oxygen starvation as blood circulation is cut off. Frostbite is painless. The nerves usually signal for some time that the part is cold, but freezing apparently prevents pain by numbing the nerves, and the only sensation is that the body part is very cold. All snowshoers have cold hands and/or feet some of the time, so it is necessary to check visually for frozen areas. Frostbitten skin is chalky white and the flesh is hard to the touch.

Treatment is to restore circulation by thawing the part. Mild surface frostbite—frost nip—often can be thawed by contact with warm flesh. Frost nip when thawed immediately does not damage the tissues. The tissue may eventually turn brown or blister as from a burn when frozen deeper. Blisters will heal readily unless they are broken and scraped or rubbed, or become infected. Heavy drainage from blisters on a frozen foot or hand that has been thawed will soak up a lot of dressings. Try to keep the area clean; makkeshift dressings can be sterilized by scorching over a flame.

Freezing a hand or foot solid is more serious. Treatment is the same but more difficult due to the extent of the injury. Thawing is done very gently without any rubbing or abrasion. Contrary to the time-honored fallacy, *do not rub* by hand or with snow as this will tear the blistered flesh and increase damage.

A sheltered place such as a tent, snow cave, or igloo is desirable as working space. Heat water over a stove to about 105°F—just above body temperature—and put the frozen hand or foot in it. Once it is thawed, protect the part from mechanical damage (do not rub it) and especially from refreezing. Bandage and protect it carefully and elevate it to promote circulation.

Before thawing a badly frozen foot the whole situation must be evaluated. Once thawed, the victim must not walk out, as pain and tissue damage will be very serious; sled or helicopter evacuation is necessary. However, if evacuation is impossible, and the choice is either to walk out or to sit for perhaps days in a very poor spot, then walk out before the extremity is thawed. Of course, the longer the part is frozen, the greater tissue damage from oxygen starvation will be, but this may be the lesser of two evils. The decision will have to be made on the spot.

Bearpawing along the Falling Waters Trail in New Hampshire's White Mountains

Be extremely careful of baring the hands or fingers to manipulate a metal object in subzero temperatures. The cold metal is an excellent conductor of heat from one's fingers—people have gotten frostbitten fingers from picking the car key out of the snow. Also, the metal will freeze to your skin, which will tear when you try to pull away. Be careful, too, when strapping on crampons or handling a stove or fuel bottle. Don't spill subzero fluids such as fuel on your fingers: this is a quick way to get frostbitten. One snowshoer I camped with insisted on a mouthwash to freshen his morning breath, forgetting that the fluid was well below freezing. Fortunately the temperature was not below zero or he would have had frostbite in his mouth.

Sunburn and Windburn

A day, or even a few hours, of sunshine is so delightful in winter that snowshoers may forget its devastating effects on exposed human flesh, particularly when compounded with reflection from snow—and both effects are made worse at elevations above 8000 feet. People have even burned the inside of their nostrils or the roof of their mouth. Be sure to carry adequate sun cream or cover with clothing as necessary.

Equally painful is windburn, which must be prevented by wearing a facemask.

Wind Chill and Overheating

Wind chill factor plays a prominent part in both hypothermia and frostbite. Wind gives the effect of a colder temperature than the thermometer shows. For example, 15°F with a 20-mph wind is equivalent to a temperature of –17°F with no wind. Mountains and ridges do queer things with wind currents. In a sheltered place you may be warm and comfortable while a hundred feet away a steady wind is blowing and another person is miserable. Clothing should be adaptable to quickly meet changing conditions.

Avoid exposing the bare hands for any length of time at low temperatures. A few minutes of subzero temperature with wind is sufficient to turn a nose or cheek white with frost nip. Use a snowshoe binding that does not require removal of mitts. Learn to strap on crampons and close zippers while wearing mitts (a length of cord tied on the zipper pull makes a hold large enough to grab with mitts or gloves). Learn to snap photos with mitts on; many Himalayan climbers have frosted their fingers when taking pictures on summits and in their befuddled state of mind did not notice until too late that their fingers would not bend.

Put safety cord on your heavy mitts. One method is to tie a cord to the cuff of each, long enough to be strung around the back of the neck. Attach another cord across your chest to the first cord; when pack is removed, cord and mitts can't fall off and be blown away by the wind.

A second method is to use a foot-long cord attached to each mitt with a piece of Velcro® or a piece of cloth with a buttonhole in it attached to the end of the cord, and a second piece of Velcro® or a button sewed on the parka sleeve between cuff and elbow. The cords are a nuisance on a bushwhack but the advantage of having them handy in windy subzero weather and not having the problem of stowing them in the pack is worth the trouble.

If your hands are easily chilled, take special care of them. Warm them under armpits—your own or a companion's—before they become dangerously cold. (Some people condition their hands to adapt to the cold by intentionally leaving mitts off as much as possible when working outdoors between winter outings.) Be prepared to cover your face if necessary; wind on the bare face can be painful even if it is not causing frostbite. Don't gasp for breath and risk frostbite in the lungs, mouth, and windpipe.

With a little careful checking you can discover at home whether you are protected from wind. Start at the bottom. The first gap is between boots and pants. You should have tie-down cuffs or gaiters, plus wind pants. Next is the pants-to-shirt gap; a short shirttail won't stay in when you are carrying a pack or bending over. The underwear or undershirt should cover the gap if the shirt doesn't. The wind parka and the insulated jacket should extend down to the mid-thigh.

The abdomen and stomach should be protected well, as this is the heat-generating center. Next the neck and face: can wind and down parka hoods be cinched up tight to leave only nose and goggled eyes out? If not, better make some adjustment. The second layer of protection is the cap-face mask, which you should be able to tuck under the lower edge of the goggles. It should cover nose and mouth and extend down the neck below the shirt collar.

For winter the goggles should have side protection. A cold wind blowing ice particles under ordinary sunglasses and across the eyeballs will have much the same effect as snow blindness (sunburn on the surface of the eyes). Check the wrists: can parka sleeves be pulled down to cover the wrist of the wool mitts and sealed with elastic cuffs? This is desirable, as it is sometimes hard to keep overmitt gauntlets high enough on the forearm to protect the wrist, where the large artery carries warming blood to the hand.

There are a variety of personal styles of dressing for severe wind chill. For example, some women wear a light balaclava to cover cheeks and chin whenever they are out in winter. When walking into the wind of Mt. Washington in New Hampshire at 0°F, a heavy balaclava may be worn on top of the light one, with hood cinched uptight and goggles on to protect the eyes.

In contrast to wind chill is overheating on sheltered slopes. Cooling is desirable to limit sweating, which dampens clothing and cuts its insulating value. When you are down to wool pants and shirt, there isn't much more you can remove, although occasionally a T-shirt is enough in a sheltered area, even at 0°F, when you are really snowshoeing hard.

Roll shirtsleeves up, unbutton the shirt, and put mitts and cap in the pack. This opens up neck, head, and wrists—where there are lots of arteries—as well as the chest and belly, to cool air. Some people use fishnet T-shirt and drawers, and unbuttoning the shirt or pants with this string garment underneath does promote cooling. Pants cuffs can be rolled up unless you will kick too much snow onto your socks. Some people put a 12-inch zipper in the seam of their pants above the knee. This can be opened for more ventilation.

Blisters

Snowshoe bindings cause a lot of blisters, especially when the boot is soft and flexible and does not take the pressure of the binding. Since the weight, when picking up the snowshoe to take a step, is on the top of the toes, this is an area that blisters often. Heels suffer on steep sidehills or when climbing steep slopes. Since snowshoes cannot be edged effectively, you must walk as on crampons, with the snowshoe flat on the sloping surface and a bend in your ankle. This is not only tiring but puts a lot of pressure on the side and back of the heel and on the heel bones.

Take lots of adhesive tape, moleskin or adhesive foam, and a few bandaids. Cover tender areas with moleskin or tape before they blister. As soon as a tender place develops, stop and perform first aid. If you use moleskin be sure to take a small scissors or a knife to cut it to fit. After sticking it on, add some strips of adhesive tape to help hold it in place. Once in a while the edge works loose and forms a lump, which makes another blister. If the blister has formed, drain it carefully with a sterile needle and apply moleskin and tape, or apply protection to relieve the pressure and leave the blister to dry up. Be careful when you remove the adhesive material at home so it doesn't pull off a large piece of live skin attached beyond the blister. Apply disinfectant if the blister has been abused in this manner.

If the blister is due to a rough spot on the inside of a heavy leather boot, carefully carve the lump with a wood chisel until it is smooth. Smooth all the wrinkles on your socks as you put your boots on, especially when you wear two or more pairs. Check for lumps in the socks, which may be wads of lint.

Stomach Upsets

Some people on week-long summer backpacks experience some form of mild stomach upset, either vomiting or diarrhea. Both these can be caused by salmonella from spoiled food residues on cooking pots "going bad." As more people crowd popular recreation sites, coliform and other microbes pollute water supplies. Winter and its cold temperatures protect the backpacker from some of these problems as living organisms in food residues and water are more or less on hold until it warms up and they can multiply profusely again. Regardless of the season, do not drink from streams. Clean, melted snow, however, is safe to drink. Still, it's best to be prepared. Making several nocturnal dashes from tent to latrine is bad enough in summer, but when it's below zero and breezy and you're camped on a glacier at 9000 feet with no sheltering trees, it's enough to try one's soul.

Some simple medication doesn't weigh very much in the pack and can help relieve these most uncomfortable problems. Kaopectate®, Alka Seltzer®, aspirin, and milk of magnesia will help with the stomach turmoil. Also, a pair of down or polyester tent bootees with leather or rubber soles are a lot faster to get into than double boots when you're in desperate straits. These light boots are quite adequate for a 50-foot dash from the tent—provided you aren't camped on a steep, icy slope. For those who require regular nocturnal strolls, the women are pretty much out of luck, but men can use an extra water bottle (preferably with a special label on it) that has a wide mouth and tight lid—with practice and skill, it will double as a urinal inside the sleeping bag.

Altitude Sickness

People suffer a myriad of miseries when exerting strenuously at elevations that are high in comparison to their home altitude. Usually the first symptom is fatigue much earlier in the hike than expected, accompanied by hard breathing. Continuing on to increased elevation will likely produce nausea and vomiting and may progress to headache and faintness.

The basic problem is lack of oxygen, and the problem will usually become noticeable after a thousand feet of elevation gain or around 10,000 to 11,000 feet. The most effective treatment is to rest or return to a lower elevation. It takes about two weeks to acclimatize from a near-sea-level altitude to the over-10,000-foot elevations.

So the treatment is to quit doing what is making you sick before you are really miserable. Slow down and don't move so fast that your lungs can't supply enough oxygen to the muscles.

CHAPTER 12

Snow Camping

More care and planning are needed for snow camping than for dry ground camping, which can be as simple as rolling the sleeping bag out under a tree, crawling into it, and going to sleep. Winter camping usually involves a group no smaller than four to six because it takes this many people to break trail for several miles in rough country when conditions are less than ideal.

Shelter

It might seem that digging a snow cave or building an igloo rather than carrying a tent would save time and energy. But considerable skill and work are necessary to create a snow shelter equal to a lightweight, roomy, modern tent, and snow in the quantity and consistency required cannot be counted on anyway. The snow cave and igloo really are not practical unless you intend to use them for more than one night or have plenty of time and energy and just want to experiment. Half an hour is plenty of time not only to set up a four-person tent but to get all four in it and supper started. Two hours of hard digging is a minimum for a four-person cave or igloo by people with average skill; realistically, three hours will probably elapse before you can expect to move in. The self-sufficient party has a larger margin of safety. If conditions prevent reaching the camping area desired, or if you get to the right area but the shelter is buried and cannot be found, or you cannot dig your cave or construct an igloo, you still must have shelter. Tents have to be the first choice, especially in somewhat unfamiliar country.

A large tent often provides shelter at low per-person weight. If three two-person tents are used, the weight of tents is from 12 to 15 pounds total, over two pounds per person; if rain flies are added, the total weight is almost three pounds per person. An eight-pound, four-person tent and a four-pound two-person tent average two pounds per person. Four people can set up the larger tent about as fast as two people can set up their two-person tent. When conditions are serious, a tarp or tent can shelter double or triple the number of people it was designed to contain.

Knowledge of the area you are going to be in is really helpful. Some excellent camp spots may not have room for a large tent, but small tents can be fitted in quite well. Although tents have drawbacks, the 8- to 14-pound weight of a roomy tent for four isn't that hard to carry, and the ease and speed of setting it up tip the scales in favor of the tent rather than the snow cave or igloo, unless the snow shelters are necessary because the location of camp is so windswept that only the most rugged expedition-model tent could survive. For the average snowshoer these tents are too heavy, expensive, and limited in usefulness (see chapter 5 for more information on tents).

Anchoring the tent ropes in snow can be quite a problem. In forested areas it is easy to find a few pieces of dead branch for tent stakes. Without this aid, be sure to carry your own stakes, about ½ × 12-inch dowel, or wood split like kindling. Place these through the loops sewn on the tent, or on the ropes, press or stamp into the snow, and pack snow over them. These small "dead men" are very secure. At times rocks exposed by wind can be used for anchors, although usually such places are too windy for a comfortable camp; the wind popping the fabric interrupts sleep.

Snowshoes and skis also make solid anchors for tent ropes—unless you need them to move around on. At times the snow is so soft that snowshoes are needed to move anywhere outside the tent. Packing the tent platform may be a job too. After you carefully pack with snowshoes and level the place to pitch the tent, you remove the webs and sink in to the knee. Then you pack the platform again by foot. But if you step off the twice-packed spot, you sink in to the hip.

If it is windy and snow is blowing it is necessary to seal the door and put up with condensation. Completely waterproof fabrics in this situation prevent any moisture from passing through the fabric and can cause near-rainfall conditions within the tent. Enough snow to wet the top of your bag can blow in through a zipper that is not completely closed.

Camping in wet weather in winter may seem foolish, but it may happen unplanned. The weather may be sunny when you start out, but before the day is over a storm moves in, yet you have to stay the night. Too, the storm may pass through and the next day will be fine. Sometimes it may be cloudy and wet in the valleys, but up high, above 10,000 feet, the weather is cold and clear. Then it is practical to put up with a day or two of storm to get to the higher scenic area where it's sunny and dry. There are times when some of the group are so ardent there is no way to talk them out of starting on the trip even in near-blizzard conditions. Only when they are sufficiently wet, cold, and miserable do they accept the fact that an outing in a winter storm truly can be worse than no outing at all.

Snow caves provide the maximum protection from storm but are time-consuming and tiring to construct. The usual problem is that the excavators get tired before there is really enough room to be comfortable. It's a bad day when you must dig your first cave ever and spend the night in it—and it is 8:00 P.M. and dark before you start.

Obviously careful thought must be given the location for a snow cave so nothing will fall on it and snow won't drift over and seal you in. During a Mountain Rescue training session in the southern Washington Cascades, some participants decided to dig their caves on the lee side of a ridge. The windward side was packed too hard, besides having a wind and drifting problem. The lee slope was not steep, it leveled out below, and it was out of the wind, so a whole string of caves was started side by side to house 30 or more persons. Real progress was being made, as the snow was deep, soft enough to dig well, but not so soft that a cave roof would fall in. To the surprise of the entire group, the slope avalanched; the tunneling had cut loose a slab avalanche, which carried the Mountain Rescue people a short distance down the slope. Among the many things to be considered in the location of the caves, avalanche hazard was the only thing overlooked in this otherwise ideal spot. If you have a choice between a flat spot sheltered by trees or an open slope where the digging is easy, be sure to consider avalanche hazard before deciding to spend the night on the slope.

Two items are handy for actual construction: a snow

shovel and either a snow saw or a folding pruning saw. An excellent shovel can be made by cutting off the blade of an aluminum grain scoop shovel so it is 12 inches long; if longer it will hold too much snow. Small aluminum snow shovels are poor tools for digging a snow cave but will suffice in the absence of the heavier grain scoop shovel. A folding pruning saw is lightweight and in some instances can be used to cut through an ice layer that the shovel cannot dent.

Carry good rain gear and extra mitts and rubber gloves in anticipation of this wet job. A group of us once built a cave for four in a blizzard at temperatures of 15°F to 20°F. We became quite wet while out of the wind working in the hole, but the moisture in our parkas froze as we traded positions and went back out in the wind; the ice made a windproof garment and discomfort was minimal.

Some locations are less satisfactory than others for snow caves, a flat place being the worst. First a hole must be excavated straight down. When the hole is deep enough—six feet or so—one person must tunnel in horizontally for the room while someone else tosses the snow up out of the original hole. A slope is useful because the snow dug out falls out of the way. Usually some of the last of it must be thrown out by a second person because as the cave reaches a depth of six to eight feet the shovel operator cannot throw the chunks out beyond the entrance. A snowshoe makes an excellent tool for the second shoveler.

There is a real technique to digging that far into snow. Of course, the snow depth must be a foot or more deeper than the cave is high—too shallow a roof, less than 12 to 18 inches, may collapse. The snow at the bottom and rear of the cave may have settled so that the shovel can be jabbed only a couple of inches into it. Then each chunk must be chipped loose on three sides and pried off the wall. Too much pressure can easily bend cheap, lightweight, aluminum shovels, which must have been designed to merely paw loose snow around. However, it is possible to study the mechanics of the problem and develop a technique to dislodge the most material with the least effort without breaking the shovel. A shortened grain scoop is quite strong and superb for this job. This is digging at its worst, reaching overhead as well as underfoot and working in awkward positions. Even more discouraging is encountering a stump or mound of dirt that forces excavation in a different direction.

It is much better to find a slope and tunnel straight in. Some diagrams show a very low opening with a high domed room beyond (Figure 27). The problem with this design is digging through the small opening on your knees or lying down. For speed, make the door high enough to dig in a fairly comfortable stance. Snow caves need plenty of ventilation, which the high door provides. Take a small plastic or nylon tarp to hang in the doorway. This will be adequate to keep the weather out unless there is a real storm raging, in which case you may want to develop a deeper, more elaborate cave.

The cave is different from a tent in that you cannot bulge the wall out with an elbow or shoulder. If the wall is touched, snow trickles down onto sleeping bags or clothing. Foam pads are the best insulation on the floor. Some pads are so light in weight that you may be tempted to carry several to better cover

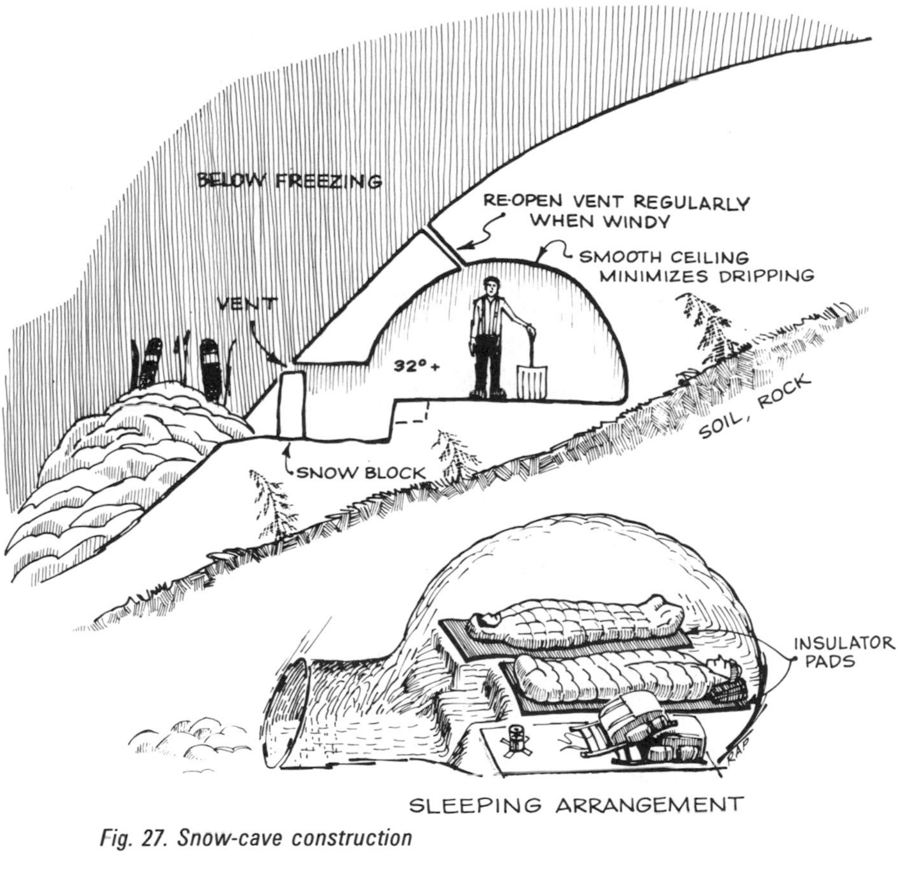

Fig. 27. Snow-cave construction

the floor of the cave, which somehow always turns out to be lumpy and hard.

Self-inflating air mattresses give a superb cushion to the otherwise surprisingly hard snow floor. However, for subzero temperatures it is usually necessary to add some insulation to the mattress. They are not as warm as a three-eighths-inch foam pad.

Once in a while it is possible to spend enough time with a good shovel to dig a cave with plenty of elbow, sleeping, and cooking room. The first such luxurious cavern I observed had a very low entrance so all heat was trapped in the smoothly domed chamber. But the instructional diagram had showed no vent hole. As supper was cooked on the gas stove, the oxygen became exhausted to the extent that the one heavy smoker in the group nearly fainted. Realizing the cause, all bailed out and soon recovered. A hole was poked through the ceiling, releasing some warmth along with carbon dioxide, carbon monoxide, and various cooking odors, and admitting oxygen.

A cave such as this is a luxury, since sounds such as wind

Fig. 28. One-person cave for shallow snow depth. Stomp snow first, then excavate 1, 2, and 3. Join caves, leaving dividing arches intact. Fill entrances to 1 and 2; close entrance to 3, with pack and plastic.

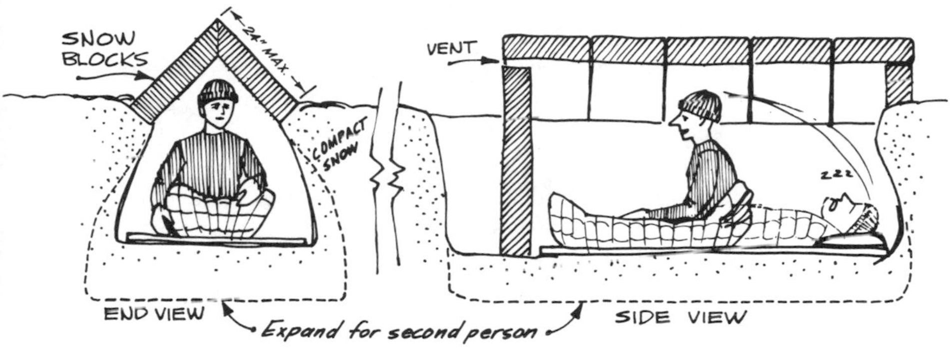

Fig. 29. One- or two-person covered trench

are stilled, giving a real sense of security to those within. Not all sounds are muted, however. Another cave I occupied had several drawbacks. The first was that we had not intended to dig it, but the February snow was so deep that we could not find the Forest Service shelter we had intended to use. So we dug a cave in a flat area because there was no convenient slope. We also dug into a tree and left a branch sticking out from one wall, which dripped water onto one sleeping bag all night. Trees outside were so loaded with snow from the storm that from time to time a branch would droop low and the immense snow load would slide off, landing with a loud whoomp! At intervals this muffled thud would awaken me so I could consider the difficulty of digging out of a collapsed snow cave. The task would probably have been impossible with several feet of snow packed around me and the sleeping bag zipped up to my nose. Simpler one-person caves and the trenches are shown in Figures 28 and 29.

Igloos are equal in protection to snow caves but more than equal in the skill required to construct them (Figure 30). They are also more subject to snow conditions. Wet, packing snow has the advantage that the blocks stick together and stay in place well, but they are quite heavy. Often there are weak layers that make it hard to cut large blocks. Wind-packed dry snow is the easiest to work with. Weight is not excessive and even large blocks are strong, do not break easily, and are easy to lift.

Often an area of dry snow must be packed with snowshoes before it can be cut into blocks. Walk it down evenly, then eat lunch and allow it 20 to 30 minutes to age harden. Don't try for more compaction by removing snowshoes as bare boots will punch holes and pack it unevenly, causing poor quality in blocks. A beginner with even, consistent blocks to work with can construct a good-looking, solid igloo.

Under ideal conditions an expert can whip up a four-person structure in about half an hour. As with a snow cave, any snow butcher with a minimum of skill and enough persistence can build an igloo. Generally allow three hours or so for the job unless you have perfected your skill through practice. Two snow saws speed the work—one for the person cutting blocks and the other to carefully tailor each block to fit the two surfaces it will touch. A shovel is also helpful; if only one saw is available, a shovel can be used for either cutting blocks or fitting them. Some people prefer a carpenter's saw to either snow saw or shovel.

One expert igloo builder advises a homemade snow saw of the following specifications: use a piece of tempered 7075 aluminum alloy about ⅛ inch thick, 2 inches wide, and 26 inches long. Attach a wooden handle to one end, leaving 20 inches for the cutting blade. Use a hacksaw to cut serrations in it for the teeth. This allows you to cut blocks up to 20 inches high, making it possible to dome over the igloo roof in about four tiers of blocks.

Cut the first tier at a slant so that the second tier will spiral up. Cut the door out after the wall is somewhat above it, since it is hard to cut out a block long enough to extend across the door opening and strong enough to support the wall above. Bevel the top of each tier inward to slope the walls inward toward the top of the dome. (Actually, a cone-shaped igloo, with nearly straight walls, is easier to construct than a rounded dome.) If the top of each tier is horizontal, you will end up with nearly vertical sidewalls and have trouble drawing them in to close the top. The person laying blocks must work within the circle as the tiers rise. Some prefer to cut blocks from the floor, excavating a foot or more of depth, which cuts down on the height of blocks to be laid. Ideal size for the blocks is about 12 by 18 by 6 inches. Uniformity is more dependent on the skill of the block cutter than the condition of the snow, but the more uniform the size and shape of the blocks, the easier it is to lay them in position.

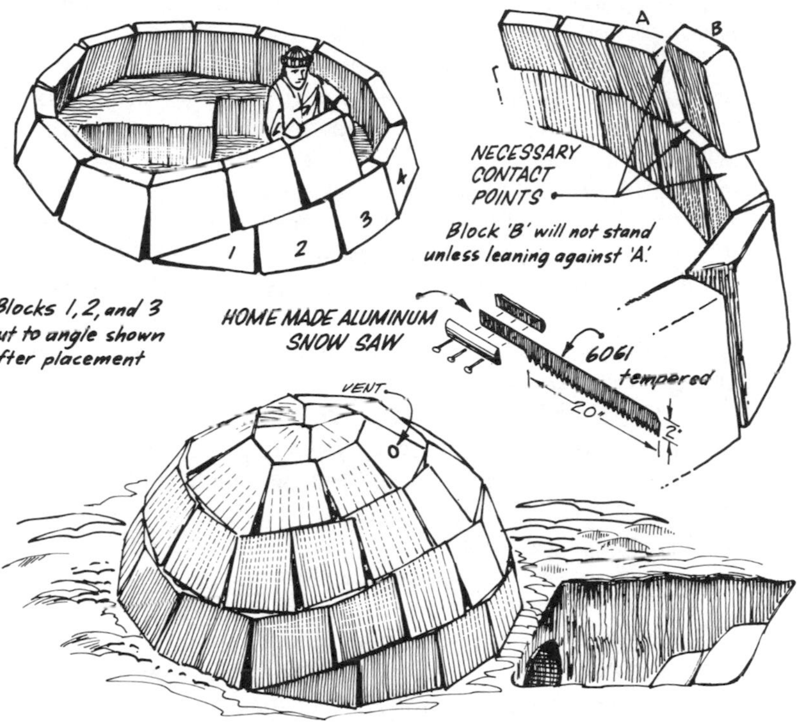

Fig. 30. Constructing a three- or four-person igloo

Layers, especially of ice, in the snow can cause blocks to come apart. Don't try to build too high, as it is difficult to fit a block if you must raise it much above shoulder level. The keystone, or capstone, block must leave an opening for ventilation; this is less of a problem than in a snow cave but still necessary. People with less than expert skill usually have no problem with ventilation. Poorly fitted blocks leave holes that make the igloo look like a Halloween Jack-o'-lantern with lots of eyes and mouths.

As in snow caving, rubber gloves are useful; long gauntlets will keep snow from working into the cuffs of your sleeves as the last blocks are raised to position. All chinks must be caulked. With powder snow it may be desirable to melt water and splash some on any weak places. An entrance tunnel may be built, although most people are ready to quit before then. A plastic tarp may be rigged to cover the opening, especially if held in place by packs on the inside.

The inside surface must have no points from which moisture can drip. The greatest disadvantage of snow shelters becomes obvious when temperatures rise above freezing. The ceiling drips, especially at the top of the door and the vent hole. The humid air may be saturated by vapor from boiling water, stove emissions, and the breath of the occupants. The interior of the igloo is illuminated by light filtering through; if light is visible through the ceiling of a snow cave, it is too thin and may fall in. The white walls of both cave and igloo reflect light so well that one flashlight or candle is usually adequate for lighting.

Other types of snow shelters include a dug trench roofed with snowshoes or dead branches and a tarp and covered with snow. Long snow blocks may be tilted together to roof over the trench (Figure 29). It is a good idea to be familiar with several of these shelters. In some places and conditions where it is impossible to use one type, another will work.

The permanent log and stone shelters erected by the Forest Service or Park Service are excellent in winter, providing protection that cannot be matched by tents or snow shelters. However, tents should be carried on backpacks to distant backcountry or high, isolated peaks even though there may be a permanent shelter at the desired camp spot. Sometimes conditions—storm, rugged snowshoeing, or delays due to people—prevent a party from reaching the shelter location. Without tents the unintentional overnight bivouac may be a real disaster.

No matter how fast you can put the tent up, dig the cave, or build the igloo, allow plenty of time for the job. Tent ropes become tangled; the weather and/or snow may be uncooperative. Winter days are short. At 47° north latitude the sun sets at 3:30 P.M. during the dark, dismal season of late December to mid January. Heavy cloud cover further cuts the limited daylight available, and some deep valley bottoms have no direct sunlight from mid November until early February.

Be aware of these damp, cold spots and prepare for them. Cold air settles to the valley bottoms in such shaded areas. Sometimes it is much warmer a hundred feet or so up the south-facing hillside. It may be worthwhile to make a short climb out of the valley bottom to camp in a warmer spot. The most ideal summer camping spot will be the place to avoid in the winter—summer campers want a cool spot and winter campers want a warmer one.

Fires

For emergencies and in lowland forest areas where dead trees abound, a fire may be a possibility during snow camping. In many areas trees are scarce and scenic and should not be used unless it really is an emergency and life, rather than comfort, depends on a fire. Starting a fire in winter is not always easy, and again preparation is the key. Practice on day hikes. Carry a piece of candle, a fire starter made of rolled newspaper soaked in paraffin wax for canning, or pitch wood. Break off a good supply of small dead twigs from near the bottom of a tree trunk; these are usually kept dry by sheltering live branches above. Occasionally you may find a dead tree with an abundance of dry dead branches, but this is rare. Ignite a pile of twigs with the fire starter and add larger pieces of wood, being careful to keep the flame going. A fuzz stick—a dry piece of wood with shavings carved in it—is an alternative where dry twigs are unavailable. A fire-resistant platform must be provided to keep the fire from melting down into the snow. A piece of light sheet metal, hinged to fold small enough to fit in the pack, is ideal. It may be suspended above the snow by baling wire attached to trees or stakes driven into the snow. Cut green wood to build the fire on only in case of an emergency to actually save a life, as living trees are too valuable to cut and burn for a mere marshmallow roast. A length of plastic or rubber tubing is an old standby that is handy for blowing on the kindling to provide a draft. The extended draft gives the flame a boost and saves the face from soot and the lungs from inhaling smoke.

If you can get some flames started in an area about six inches across, the fire will probably go. By the time the flames are a square foot in extent with a good bed of coals, good-size pieces of fairly wet wood may be added, and the heat will dry them and continue burning. Sometimes desperate methods must be used—such as carrying a pint of gasoline, a highway flare, or a half pound of old inner tube—to get the blaze going. Many outdoor manuals show solid tablets of fuel and other fire starters. But for real performance under difficult circumstances these are inadequate for the job at hand.

Most sure-fire aids are as heavy as a stove. It is usually hard to get a fire going under winter conditions, even when fairly dry dead branches or dry twigs are available. At times it may be impossible because moisture in the air has saturated even dead wood. Some areas just do not have enough firewood for the number of people who camp there. Generally it is not practical or desirable to depend on using a wood fire. But don't let the old time woodsman skill at starting a fire die out. An emergency may arise when a huge heat source such as a generous bonfire would mean surviving well for several days.

Stoves and Cooking

Although open fires are not practical in a snow cave or igloo, cooking over a stove in a tent or snow cave is not easy either. Extra care must be taken to clear a place large enough to set up the stove. Any spillage of fuel or food lands on the sleeping bags or on the floor, making frequent house-cleaning necessary. For this reason it is a good idea to use a simple menu for meals when conditions such as storm or extreme cold or a predawn start make it necessary to cook inside the shelter.

The greatest problem in tent housekeeping is melting snow for water. A large pot is necessary to hold the necessary volume of snow. Potential disasters develop when a gallon of water is perched on top of a half-pint stove, especially when the ingredients for dinner have been added. Dumping snow in the pot usually leaves some dribbles of snow from the tent door to the pot on the stove. Dipping hot water from the container adds more drops to the tent floor. If the stove is set on the floor without an insulating pad or piece of plywood under it, melting snow underneath may slowly tip the water pot off the burner.

A coated-nylon stuff sack large enough to hold a sleeping bag and with no leaks can make the snow-melting process easier. Fill the sack with snow, brush off all the snow on the outside of it, and bring it into the tent or shelter. Snow can then be carefully ladled into the melting pot with minimum spillage and only one trip outside for snow.

Certain techniques are learned when cooking over a small stove in cramped quarters. Limited heat on a single burner dictates that one course be prepared and consumed at a time. The time and bother in melting snow for water generally prompts people to choose a one-course, one-dish meal. In its simplest form, snow is melted and the water is heated and poured into individual containers to reconstitute some dehydrated or freeze-dried food. More snow is added to the pot, and by the time the food is eaten, more hot water is available. If someone is still hungry, another round is fixed, and more snow added to the pot. As each person finishes eating, the hot water is used for cocoa, tea, powdered juice mix, or coffee to rinse the food residue from the cup.

The vast variety of dehydrated foods available since World War II has gained immense popularity. Replacing the traditional can of pork and beans, the new foods are lightweight, simple, and fast to reconstitute. Cost is quite high, especially when the items are packaged in individual servings. Directions must be read carefully, as some require only the addition of boiling water and others are best when added to another ingredient. Still others must be soaked in one kettle and then fried; read the labels carefully at home to be sure to take along enough utensils.

Great progress has been made in saving weight, but despite the exotic names on the package, the flavor is uniformly drab and monotonous without additional seasoning. Backpackers have little choice, as the alternative are prohibitive weight or starvation. But cold temperatures and availability of snow for refrigeration give snowshoers the option of including uncooked meat, frozen foods, and other perishables in the menu. However, the weight of these items is so great they are likely to be used only as a delicious respite from the processed mainstay.

Encourage ingenuity in menu planning. Mountain snowshoers have revolutionized snowshoe design and technique—it's about time someone did something about the food.

Garbage and Waste

It is easy to forget that the blanket of snow that covers all ugliness will melt away and reveal every tin can and candy wrapper left by thoughtless winter campers. The message is brief and admits no exceptions: if you can carry it in full, you can carry it out empty.

Human wastes cannot be buried in topsoil as they should be in summer, so choose as unobtrusive a location as possible, such as the depths of a clump of trees, and, whenever possible, burn the used toilet paper. (The amount of yellow snow along popular snow hikes does not enhance the backcountry beauty. Make the effort to get off the trail and out of sight.)

CHAPTER 13

Snowshoe Racing

Running on snowshoes is a popular pastime in Midwest and Eastern U.S. and Eastern Canada. Some racers run comparatively short distances—up to 1500 meters—on flat oval tracks such as those used by track and field athletes. Other races are longer distances, up to 10 and 14 miles, on a rolling or hilly course similar to that used in cross-country ski races. There's even a 100-mile Alaskan race called the Iditashoe.

At this date wood-frame, rawhide-laced snowshoes are required equipment for one group and the small metal frame Western snowshoe is preferred by a different organization. This chapter will be divided among the three regional areas which differ in equipment and style of racing.

Snowshoe racers in Quebec, Ontario, and New England race mainly by rules of the Canadian Snowshoe Union and the American Snowshoe Union. This is sometimes described as French-Canadian and Franco-American style of snowshoe racing. The unions exist partly to preserve the wood-frame, babiche (rawhide)-laced snowshoe used with the lampwick, or squaw hitch, binding. These special racing snowshoes, weighing 19 ounces, are the lightest of any used for racing. A 9×32-inch size is used for running and a 10×32-inch for race walking, or the hard walking. No cleats or traction devices are permitted on either size.

Races include runs of 50, 100, 200, 400, and 800 meters; 1500-meter, one-mile, and 10-mile hard walks; and 100-meter hurdles. Both men and women compete in several age groups, from under 20 to over 60 years of age.

Hoarfrost in the western mountains

At present there are 40 clubs within the Canadian Snowshoe Union and 20 in the American Snowshoe Union who sponsor races and social gatherings. Each club has a uniform, usually of heavy wool coat and pants, with distinctive colors and names. Sweat clothes and running shoes are accepted clothing for meets. Previously, racers wore heavy club uniform and mocassins.

Representatives of the Canadian and American snowshoe unions make up the International Snowshoe Union. This body establishes the rules for international competition, including the number and location of such events each year, and resolves any disputes or disagreements.

As many as 1200 people have attended the International Snowshoe Convention, a yearly meet and festival held alternately in Canada and the U.S. The approximately 250 race participants must qualify in previous meets.

The races are usually held on somewhat prepared courses—often snow-covered running tracks—packed down or churned up depending on the temperature and type of snow. When the convention was held in Ottawa in 1975, streets were closed for the race course and snow trucked in because a warm spell had bared the pavement.

A major item of business each year for all organized snowshoe racing is adapting to the weather. When snow falls early and stays on the ground a long time, more meets will be scheduled. A shortened racing season will be caused by poor snow cover—or no snow at all. Sometimes the snow melts off early, in which case races may be run on last year's dead grass. Racing is more sensitive to lack of snow than recreational snowshoeing. Mountain heights receive more snow than valley floors, but you can't move these races to mountain ridges and summits!

For more information about the Canadian Snowshoe Union and the American Snowshoe Union, write to their representatives at the addresses listed at the end of this chapter.

A somewhat different style of racing on snowshoes is done in the upper Midwest: Wisconsin, Michigan, and Minnesota. Local community races have been held for years, and an 80-mile race sponsored by a distillery has created even more interest.

Long, snowy winters and cold temperatures are nearly

synonymous with this region. The midwest style of racing is less structured than that of other racing groups in regard to equipment and length of races. Longer distances on a cross-country ski course are the norm.

The midwestern races are run in Western snowshoes that are a minimum size of 8 × 25 inches. Because of the soft snow on many courses, racers often use larger snowshoes. At times snowshoe races are run on packed snow that is nearly as hard as ice, where a runner without snowshoes would be faster. However, the 4.5- and 9.5-mile races are about half on groomed cross-country courses and half through the woods and up and down hills. Sometimes there is trail breaking, and a snowshoe is necessary to keep from sinking deeply. The annual meet at Wausau, Wisconsin, is at present the main scheduled event in this area.

In 1977 a group of people near the Adirondack Mountains of New York organized to promote snowshoe racing. The United States Snowshoe Association (USSSA) has had remarkable success in popularizing racing, helping to make it a medal event in the annual Empire (New York) State Winter Games.

The USSSA races were run on 300-meter oval tracks. The preferred snowshoe is the 8 × 25-inch Western of aluminum tubing and synthetic decking, with traction cleat and heavy-duty binding.

Paul Smith's College in the northern Adirondacks has continued the 100-, 200-, and 400-meter sprints, plus the 1500-meter race walk that the now defunct USSSA started. Their main event is at Gabriels, New York, and racers from the Canadian Snowshoe Union, wearing wood snowshoes, join them. This meet is called the North American Snowshoe Classic.

A few weeks later the American racers journey to Hull, Quebec, just across the river from Ottawa, Ontario, for the final meet of the Canadian season. In French-speaking Quebec the event is called the Classique Nord Americaine De La Raquette. The Empire State Winter Games at Lake Placid, New York, is a major event, with skiing, skating, and snowshoe races. It is held in late winter annually.

As if running on snowshoes at sea level isn't hard enough, now a roster of races is scheduled in Colorado at 10,000 feet or so. Some races are short sprints, while a growing number are longer distances. In a way this is appropriate as snow doesn't

Mt. Stuart from Ingalls Pass

lend itself to high-speed travel except downhill on skis. The long-term ethic for races on snow seems to be more in the nature of long distances and endurance.

At present people with a spring, summer, and fall habit of running or jogging have discovered small, lightweight snowshoes, and now can train and compete year-round. People with a long-term running obsession are into races of several miles rather than sprints of a couple hundred meters.

The stress of running in cold weather is no drawback to people who love running and competing. I entered the 1500-meter race walk at the 1991 North American Snowshoe Classic at Gabriels, New York. At age 62 I was 20 years older than the next oldest racer, so was obviously no threat to anyone.

Warming up before training or competing is of the greatest importance, as cold muscles are easily strained or torn. I used lots of hot ointment on my thighs, mainly hamstrings, and thus reeked like an athletic dressing room in the "olden days." Present-day exercise rooms are more into perfume and deodorant than horse liniment.

Of the seventeen people—male and female—in my race, only two or three were serious athletes. The rest were of varying degrees of speed, and seven were less serious or speedy than this old farmer! This seems to be fairly typical of most such races. The socializing with people from the opposite side of the continent was more rewarding than the athletic achievement.

Snowshoe racing is a totally different kind of snowshoeing from that done during hiking and backpacking in the mountains. A westerner would never run out of new mountain areas to snowshoe. However, the limited extent of eastern mountains causes the local snowshoers to repeat climbs, sometimes frequently. One very active snowshoer has been up all the New England 46 summits over 4000 feet in elevation in winter, and is nearing ascending each from all four points of the compass in winter. It's not surprising that snowshoe racing has developed in the Midwest and East, where winters are very long and subzero temperatures would tend to discourage the backpacker from camping out in the backcountry.

The nearest thing to snowshoe racing in Washington State has been some winter mountain-rescue practices. Several have been sponsored by Ellensburg Mountain Rescue. The simulated rescue format calls for a "victim" to be evacuated in a rescue sled off a nontechnical mountain summit (no mountaineering required), with the winning team the first to complete the roughly three-hour round trip, which includes an elevation gain of 3000 feet.

For more information on snowshoe racing contact the following organizations:

International Amateur Snowshoe Racing Federation (IASSRF)

Canadian Snowshoe Union
(Member IASSRF)
Serge Lebel
9 Beriault
Hull, Quebec, Canada
J8X 1A1

American Snowshoe Union
(Member IASSRF)
Joan Brady
625 Bridge St. #7
Lowell, MA 01850

North American Snowshoe Classic, Jim Tucker,
14 Pickett Hall, Paul Smith's College,
Paul Smith's, NY 12970

APPENDIX 1

Equipment Checklist

Many of the items in this list have not needed description in the text. By the time most people are ready to try snowshoeing, they have acquired some knowledge and equipment, and general suggestions should be adequate. If any doubt remains, further reference material can be found in the Suggested Reading List.

The following checklist is not intended to be definitive. Other items may be equally satisfactory; the last word on snowshoeing equipment has yet to be written. Try your own ideas, improvise, and modify. There is plenty of room for improvement.

Not all items need be taken on all trips. On an easy, short hike some items may be excluded. For longer hikes where a delay could force an overnight stay, start adding the items listed under Group and Optional.

Snowshoe groups usually stay together because the stronger members cannot outrun the weaker when breaking trail through deep snow. A tired person cannot be left to sit beside the trail several hours in 10°F weather so that the rest of the party can continue to the objective. Therefore some items such as map and compass may be shared within a group, and to a lesser extent, first-aid supplies. Make sure someone else has the items you plan to leave home. Even experienced people sometimes inadvertently overlook such items as matches.

Ski poles fully occupy both hands, and even with an ice axe, a headlight-type flashlight is more practical than a handheld one. Headlights that use a six-volt battery give much longer service than two-cell models and are strongly recommended. Lithium cell lights are the lightest-weight and longest-lived ones available. Cold temperature shortens battery life and short days require more flashlight use, so equip yourself better than in summer.

Add a stove per group for a hot drink during rest stops. Don't skimp on matches and fire starter if you intend to build a fire; remember that dry wood is scarce or nonexistent at this time of year. It is unwise to depend on a fire, however, as burnable wood is increasingly scarce. Carry a knife with a leather punch and add a saw to group equipment. Shovel and snow saw are optional and depend on the length of the trip and risk of an overnight stay on one-day trips.

Extra food is of less importance because the risk of starvation during an overnight stay is slight, but the risk of hypothermia and/or frostbite is very high if you are caught in a storm without much shelter. Most of the small emergency kits contain a tea bag, bouillon, and sugar cubes as extra food. These items won't do much to prolong life; their chief purpose is to help pass the unpleasant hours more easily and to improve the taste of wood-ash-flavored melted snow.

As you gain experience from snowshoeing in different conditions, deciding what to put in your pack will be less of a problem. Some equipment desirable on a subzero outing will not be necessary for a mid-May, 60°F hike. If there are beginners along, be sure to check that everyone has the essentials; take the time and effort to help the first-timer shake down equipment.

Plan your equipment creatively and don't depend blindly on what any checklist indicates. Improvise and experiment so that your equipment will meet the varying conditions you find in your area without unnecessary fussing and adjusting. If the gear you have doesn't work, learn to make it work or replace it. Don't spend your outdoor time changing clothes and tightening or loosening straps and buckles. Enjoy the winter backcountry to the fullest while you are there.

One-Day Hike

Clothing

Underwear

Wool or polypropylene shirt, with or without T-shirt or long-sleeve jersey

Wool or polypropylene pants with tie-down or gaiters, expedition overboots or mukluks

Wind pants or warm ups—preferably with leg zippers
Down or fiberfill parka, or down vest and dacron-filled parka
Wool or polypropylene cap and face mask or combination
Wool or polypropylene mitts and extras, or overmitts, ski mitts, or snowmobile mitts
Wool or polypropylene socks, cotton next to skin if necessary
Climbing or hiking boots or insulated boots of foam rubber, felt liners if necessary
Add for extra warmth if needed:
  Quilted down or dacron-filled jacket or sweater
  Scarf

Equipment

Snowshoes, bindings, and traction device
Ice axe with basket or ski poles
Frame pack or rucksack
Sun goggles, sun cream
Matches and fire starter
First-aid kit containing bandages, tape, moleskin or adhesive foam, scissors, bandages
Repair cord and pocket knife with leather punch
Flashlight, preferably headlight-type
Canteen or thermos
Lunch and a little extra food
Add, per group:
  Compass and map of the area—1 or 2
  Flagging—plastic or crepe paper
  Folding saw—1
  Shovels—2
  Wands with flagging attached—25 (if route is intricate or long)
  Plastic or nylon tarps—1 or 2 (for emergency overnight stay)
If weather is 10°F or colder, add or change to:
  Extra warm clothing
  Insulated warm-ups or long underwear and wind pants
  Down mitts or especially warm insulated mitts, equipped with safety cord to prevent loss in wind
  Expedition overboots over heavy climbing or double boots
  Sweater—wool, polypropylene, down, or dacron
  Stove and pot for hot drinks or heavy-duty fire starter

For avalanche country:
- Avalanche probes—1 or 2 per group
- 50 feet of eighth-inch avalanche cord
- Radio avalanche victim detectors—1 for each party member

Special for subzero outings:
- Quart water bottle with narrow neck in pack next to your back
- Quart or pint bottle with narrow neck inside shirt, equipped with neck cord for easier retrieval from shirt front (narrow neck is easier to open when water has frozen in the threads of the cap)

Extra socks and mitts

Snorkel—optional

Down-filled tent slippers—optional

Adequate sleeping bag

Foam pad

Sleeping-bag liner

Cup, spoon, and cooking utensils as needed

Hot breakfast and dinners, with hot drink

Cold lunch (optional)—stop to heat water for hot drink on trail

For the group:
- Tent or tents—adequate space for entire group
- Snow anchors
- Rainfly—optional
- Plastic or nylon tarp or large garbage sack for storing packs and gear outside if there is not enough room in tents
- Stove, extra fuel, pot large enough to melt snow
- Base for stove or metal fire platform
- Shovel, snow saw for leveling tent platform or digging cave or building igloo
- Whisk broom to brush snow off boots, etc., brought into tent

APPENDIX 2

Suggested Reading

Fear, Gene. **Surviving the Unexpected Wilderness Emergency.** Tacoma, Washington: Survival Education Association, 1972.

LaChapelle, Edward R. **The ABC of Avalanche Safety** (2nd edition). Seattle: The Mountaineers, 1985.

Lentz, Martha; Macdonald, Steven, and Carline, Jan. **Mountaineering First Aid** (3rd edition). Seattle: The Mountaineers, 1985.

Manning, Harvey. **Backpacking: One Step at a Time** (3rd edition). New York: Random House, 1980.

Peters, Ed, ed. **Mountaineering: The Freedom of the Hills** (4th edition). Seattle: The Mountaineers, 1982.

Index

Page numbers for photos and figures are in italics.

Washington 24, *48*, *70*, *105*, *112*, 117, 131–32, 133, 165

About the author:

Gene Prater, a resident of Ellensburg, Washington, was introduced to the art of snowshoeing at age 21 and has since used these webbed feet to enjoy winter hiking and ascend countless peaks. He is also a sometime designer and builder of custom snowshoes. Prater has for several years led snowshoeing seminars in New England (for the Appalachian Mountain Club), the Rockies, and the Pacific Northwest.